BURY ME IN AN OLD
PRESS BOX

Fred Russell

BURY ME IN AN OLD PRESS BOX

*Good Times
and Life of a
Sportswriter*

A. S. Barnes and Company • New York

To Kay

Foreword

A sportswriter's life, if not the purest of pleasures, is surely not to be likened to toil. I find it very difficult to make my job sound like work at all—and I promise not to dwell overlong on that aspect of sportswriting anywhere in this book, lest I spoil the outlook of any man who regards sportswriters with envy.

Such envy is not misdirected. The game we call Life got off to an unusual start, according to my reading of the most widely-published account. The Referee explained the rules; the rules got broken right off the bat; a penalty was inflicted. And what, you may ask, was unusual about that? The severity of the penalty: banishment forever from the Garden, and the guilty man would henceforth have to *work* for a living. You can look it up yourself in the Book if you don't believe me.

You can also look up *sport* in the dictionary and find that the word's original meaning was *to carry away from work*.

Doesn't this prove that sport is the best thing man has thought up since the Garden of Eden?

There's something else worth noting about the word *sport*. It is an abbreviation of *disport,* which means *to divert, to amuse, to make merry.* Let me confess: those things appeal to me.

The sports pages of a newspaper exert an appeal based on several factors that a serious fellow might think were more important than diversion, amusement and merry-making, and more deserving of first place in a sportswriter's listing of the several factors. But I believe that most people who turn to the sports page first do so because there is so little fun anywhere else in the paper. The "funnies" are not even called that anymore, and the term "comic strip" is a gross misnomer for all but a few. As for the front page, it seems eternally permeated with the perils of our position in the Middle East, arguments among politicians, automobile wrecks and bad weather. The society section does offer a view of people being nice, but the phrases are too often the same even though the names and faces may be different from day to day, and the phrases try very hard never to be funny. There are seldom any chuckles amid the business news and surveys, nor in the newspaper's helps for homemakers, nor is a good guffaw to be expected throughout the rest of the paper in enough instances to justify a thorough reading of the whole thing by a soul who needs cheering up.

Yet the soul's need for cheering up is very real; laughter is the lubrication of the spirit. Sportswriters try to meet this need more and more nowadays, and their effort is commendable although their motives are not completely unselfish. They know that if humor can be contrived, readers can be got. But this is by far the lesser cause of the comedy that can be found more easily and more often on the sports page than anywhere else in most newspapers. Sportswriters do not need to contrive humor; they can manage very well if they only put in print a good selection of the humor they see and hear in covering their beats.

Sport has always produced an inordinate lot of fun for the participants and the spectators—and by fun I mean the humorous twists and the delightful oddballs as much as I mean the over-all circumstances of happiness in which games are played and enjoyed.

As for these happy circumstances, I am sure that the most eloquently simple testimony I ever heard was Herbert Bayard Swope's. A group of old friends and associates of Grantland Rice got together a year or so after Granny's death, to ring the bells for Granny and to wring some joy out of old memories. Swope's turn came and he reminisced about his early newspaper days when he and Rice were young sportswriters going to the games and the races together. In a few words, Swope made it very clear that back yonder he had had a wonderful time. As he ended his reminiscing, he expressed his regret over having had not nearly enough opportunities to see Rice later on, after he himself quit the world of sports for other jobs. But Rice, in the opinion of his old friend, made the better choice.

"He stayed with happiness," was Swope's way of putting it.

I do not wish to claim too much for sport, nor even seem to argue for more than is its just due, lest I weaken sport's case which is a very strong one. There are more lasting varieties of happiness to be found elsewhere (in the family, to name an obvious place to look); and, in man's love for God and man (not to mention love of woman and child and home and country), there are higher degrees of happiness than sport affords.

I say that happiness is found most *readily* in sport, and more predictably, by plan, than elsewhere. Sport is a contest, physical and mental. Happiness comes out of contest, won fairly or lost honorably. "Man's greatest moment of happiness," I once heard a great man say, "is to be tested beyond what he thought might be his breaking point—and not fail."

Sport abounds in such moments.

Now back to the comedy and the clowns.

The close affinity between sport and humor is due in part, I think, to their dependence on the same principle for kicks. Call it the Principle of the Pleasant Let-down; or, to state it another way, people get such a kick out of their release from tension that they tend to seek tension (in stadiums, for instance) or deliberately create it themselves, in order to get release from it. Where would be the pleasure of taking off your shoes, if they were not too tight? Jokes do the same thing. They grasp the listener with an intriguing situation, which suddenly collapses into comedy.

There is also the special need of the athlete himself for release from the all-over kind of tension that is the enemy of top performance. He should be loose, every muscle relaxed, in order to pour all his energy and strength into just the muscles he wants, when the brain and glands command.

One of the wisest baseball men I know says, of a certain very successful manager, "Casey is a clown, but smart— smart beyond baseball. He's never funny at the wrong time."

There are any number of football coaches who actually owe their reputations as masterminds not to superior strategy or systems or even material—but to their ability to build up or relax, almost at will, the tensions of their teams. Some go about it solemnly. But some wear their funny-face nine days out of ten, and save their fierce one for when it's really necessary.

But if release from tension is necessary and desirable, what about relief of tedium? There are dull days, even in sport. Anything to relieve the tedium is good, and better if funny, and best of all if the joke serves justice by being at the expense of somebody guilty of taking himself too seriously.

An example that comes to mind was the gag contrived at a basketball tournament years ago by some sportswriters who were weary of the official timer's grim attitude generally, and particularly by the man's pompous posturing whenever he performed his little chore of firing a blank cartridge. He would take his stance unnecessarily long in advance, stopwatch held conspicuously in hand outstretched before his eyes, pistol held conspicuously in hand outstretched toward the ceiling of the gymnasium. The jokesters waited until the gun went off. From the rafters dropped, right at the man's feet, a fully-feathered, but dead, turkey.

Just as "the punishment should fit the crime," the fooling should fit the seriousness of the sin. Or should I call it sin-of-seriousness? Anyway, if no real harm was meant by the sinner, mild nonsense serves him right and very well. For illustration, I recall the case of Fresco Thompson, then scouting for the Dodgers, and a young baseball player whose sin was simply the schoolboyish stratagem of asking a question to attract attention and appear smart. The conversation went like this:

"Mr. Thompson, have you noticed my swing?" the boy asked. "I seem to be hitting under the ball."

"Why, no, I hadn't noticed," Fresco answered.

"Well, sir, I'm not meeting it quite level. I'm hitting more flies than line drives."

"How much are you hitting under the ball?"

"Oh, just a tiny bit, I figure. Like this—" and he held thumb and forefinger a sixteenth of an inch apart.

"Well, I tell you what you do. You get some inner-soles."

Pure nonsense won't get the job done if the offenders are very numerous and their sin-of-seriousness is one that constitutes a real threat to the welfare of sport. Then the humorous dart must be barbed with some truth, as in the classic utterance of Penn State's Bob Higgins:

"There are three things everybody thinks he can do better than the other fellow—build a fire, run a hotel and coach a football team."

If you will grant my first two claims—that sport is a wellspring of humor, and sport offers highgrade happiness to man on the most convenient terms available anywhere— then I move on to some other values and virtues among which, perchance, you may come across your own favorite.

How about *fairness?* I say the field of sport is a place where all of us ordinary people succeed, beyond our success anywhere else, in behaving ourselves while having fun. Where else do we always give everybody an even start and an equal number of innings at bat? Where else are the goals all attainable and set in plain view for everybody to see and strive for? Think what a fine world we would live in if, in all fields, we could rule out everything that is unfair and wrongful. That is just about what we manage to do in the field of sport, isn't it?

Sport is quick to outlaw any piece of unfairness that can be covered and controlled by a rule. Sport is slow to award its accolade, sportsmanship, and never applies it to mere observance of the letter of the law. Sportsmanship means obedience to the unenforceable.

Sportswriters have the duty of standing vigil for transgressions of sportsmanship, and there is virtually no chance for a flagrant violation of the code to go undetected and undenounced. Lately the Sportsmanship Brotherhood, Inc., has awarded a plaque every year, commemorating the fair name of Grantland Rice among sportsmen and coupling some sportswriter's name briefly with "the Grantland Rice tradition." They named me once, and I am awfully proud of the plaque.

Even the true meaning of sportsmanship, however, fails to cover another aspect of fairness that pervades sport. I call your attention to the kindly workings of the Law of Average, and to the fair distribution of talents that commonly occurs between contesting teams and individuals. Great size and great speed are very infrequently found together; the greatest size and the greatest speed, never. This is very comforting, what?

The specific case of Mickey Mantle should be cited, I think, in the very words that were splendidly applied to him by Paul Richards, who said of Mickey:

"He is the best hitter, the best runner, the best fielder, the best thrower. That's all there is."

Has this ever happened before in the whole history of baseball—superlative ability in the four facets of the game, possessed by the same player? Any exception so rare, I argue, only proves the rule.

And besides, Mickey Mantle is unequal to the pitchers more than half the times he faces them.

If you agree with the poet that variety is the very spice of life, give sport a high mark there. As the seasons of the several sports give way to the next one I am always glad. There is a perennial freshness in the face of each sport as it comes onto the calendar. There is also the natural freshness of sunshine and blue sky and green grass. And youth.

John Kieran once wrote a brief argument against the dictum that variety is the spice of life. *Enthusiasm* is, he claimed—and so named another of sport's charms. Kieran quoted Emerson: "Nothing great was ever achieved without enthusiasm"; and then stated his own point of view in this paragraph:

"I'm prejudiced in this matter because I'm full of enthusiams for and against persons, places and conditions. Many years ago, when I was on the staff of a big-city newspaper, I used to amuse one of the elder editors with almost daily impassioned pleas for or violent attacks on some matter of the moment. One day the kindly veteran said to me mildly: 'I wish I could get as excited about anything as you do about everything.' Well, it's more fun that way. An enthusiast may bore others—but he has never a dull moment himself."

On the sports page, readers are looking for excitement and enthusiasm and are never bored with it unless the writer has let his own enthusiasm mislead him to silly errors of judgment. Sportswriters are all enthusiasts. The few who try to be cynical soon get converted or quit. H. G. Salsinger (Detroit *News*) tells this story:

"We were invited to a dinner a few years ago on the night of a championship fight in New York. The dinner was set for six o'clock so that everyone could get an early start for the Yankee Stadium. None of the dozen writers could eat. They apologized to their host after the second course was served and left in a body. On the way to the stadium a veteran remarked: 'On the day when I don't feel this nervous excitement creeping over me before a big fight, or any other important event, I'm going to retire.'"

Many are embraced by the *camaraderie* of sport. Team success depends on team morale; team morale and *esprit de corps* are the same thing. However, a team can lack the winning spirit and still enjoy a high level of *camaraderie*. This is how a college football squad invariably becomes a sort of fraternity for its members while they are in college and after, whether they have won or lost on the field. The players may all belong to various Greek-letter fraternities too, but their loyalties there are apt to be lessened a little for having their need of close human support met so well at the stadium and the practice field and the locker room.

The camaraderie of the crowd at a sports event can be felt by anybody. It was responsible for the following bit of nonsense:

An inebriated fellow sitting 'way up in Row 65 got to his feet time and again and yelled, "Hey! Gus! Look here, Gus!"

Whereupon, down in Row 20 a man would rise, look up, and wave. This friendly exchange went on interminably, until finally the man down in Row 20 shouted back to the drunk and advised him to stay in his seat and look at the game. "And besides," he finished, "my name's not Gus."

Related to camaraderie is the extraordinary capacity of the audience for knowledge of sport. It is an understanding audience, as understanding as any writer could ask and far better than most writers have. Literary critics have pointed out the troubles faced by serious authors today if they rely on the classic sources for allusions and analogies. The authors cannot safely assume that their readers will recognize allusions to the King James Bible and Shakespeare or ancient history and myths. A sportswriter, however, can safely assume that most of his readers will catch the meaning of every reference he makes to the legends and heroes of sport, ancient or recent. And if he's not sure everybody will know, the sportswriter can always add a simple and unpretentious identifying phrase such as "the Cincinnati shortstop" or "oldtime Alabama halfback," without giving the appearance of parading his erudition in the manner of an author who adds "Roman Emperor" or "Hamlet's sister." We've got to remember, as somebody said not too long ago, that "In the bright lexicon of youth there is no such word as *fail*—or *lexicon*."

Let me name one more cardinal virtue of sport, and I am done with this sermonizing. The *challenge* that is always present in sport is the kind of thing implicit in the adage, "Not to have tried is the true failure." Hence we give a mighty hail to Roger Bannister when he becomes the first man in history to run the mile in less than four minutes, but we don't condemn as failures all the earlier athletes who got the record closer and closer to the magic mark but never made it under. Instead we insist that they shared in Bannister's success and contributed to it by shaving the seconds down to a point where four minutes was but the next step. Since he took that step, look at all the other runners who have raced the mile in less than four minutes!

To surpass others is a common aspiration among human beings. Sport offers opportunity, and some can succeed.

To surpass ourselves is even better, and is also a common aspiration. Sport offers opportunity wherein all can succeed.

Table Of Contents

Table Of Content

BURY ME IN AN OLD
PRESS BOX

You Gotta Be Lucky

I acquired my appreciation of the finer things of life at a very early age. On my seventh birthday I got a "King of the Diamond" baseball; instantly I knew this off-brand thing was undeniably inferior to the "Junior League" ball (horsehide with genuine rubber center) which my brother John, two years older, had received. But I didn't squawk; the gift might have been an undersized guitar or mandolin. My grandmother taught music and I had a haunting fear of being subjected to the keys and strings.

This was at Wartrace, a green and rock-fencey Tennessee town fifty miles southeast of Nashville on the main line of the railroad to Chattanooga. I would slip away to the gravel pile at the end of our street and hit pebbles with a paddle, hour after hour, right-handed and then left-handed, to avoid the threat of music lessons. I liked music—but only to listen to; I used to sleep on a green pad next to the organ in the Methodist Church when my mother played for the Sunday night services and the Wednesday night prayer meetings. There's the remembered impression of a trip to Nashville and seeing a show window full of her (Mabel

Lee McFerrin) compositions in the old H. A. French music store. But my clearest childhood recollection is of an innate taste for sports and a bent of mind to read everything that was in a newspaper.

My father, John Russell, when he was twenty-three and not yet married had started a weekly paper, the Wartrace *Tribune*. It didn't last long. He moved to Nashville in the mid-1890's and must have had a real good time of it as an assistant to William Luigart, restaurant and hotel operator. He developed a fondness for the horse racing, sports and theater atmosphere, which he forsook to move back to Wartrace because "a small town was the best place to raise children."

Many years later I discovered that the day chosen for moving, in the late fall of 1906 when I was three months old, was the day Vanderbilt played and defeated the Carlisle Indians, 4 to 0, in the South's greatest intersectional football victory up to that time. It was a dirty trick not letting me see that game. Think of all the columns I could have begun: "When I saw the Carlisle Indians. . . ."

As a salesman for a wholesale grocery company, known in those days as a "drummer," my father traveled the Middle Tennessee territory in a horse and buggy those first years. He was a collector of stories, some of them told at the dinner table each night, and of funny sayings he had heard or read. Comments by his favorite paragrapher, "Abe Martin" (Kin Hubbard), he would stick in a pigeon-hole in his roll-top desk. One I remember: "If capital and labor ever do git t'gether, it's goodnight fer th' rest of us."

This one he probably made up: "The most foresighted fellow I ever knew was a roommate I had at Terrell College (Decherd, Tenn.). He always replaced his shoestrings just before they broke."

I suppose he made good use of these with his customers. At least they laughed a lot and seemed glad to see him.

2

I can hear him now, telling a country storekeeper about a Wartrace character who was inclined to drink too much. This fellow had laid off from work and was in bed, feeling horrible. Seeking sympathy, he called his wife and asked her to kneel and pray for him. Which she did, saying: "Lord, please be easy and forgiving with Henry. He's drunk—"

"Don't tell Him I'm drunk," interrupted the husband, sorely irritated. "Tell Him I'm sick."

Any time I accompanied my dad on a trip, whether by buggy or train, it was a good bet that we would return with some kind of pet—pigeon or rooster or lamb. Always, we had a dog, and it's too bad none of them could read, for pasted on the whitewashed dog house was this clipping: "A great pleasure of a dog is that you make a fool of yourself with him and not only will he not scold you, but he will make a fool of himself, too."

On a snowy Christmas morning we might find a ladder against the house, a couple of bricks out of the chimney and some sparklers, Roman candles, oranges, English walnuts and a reindeer whip strewn near Santa Claus' footsteps. One Christmas a roller coaster extended from the front door through three rooms in our house and on to the back porch. And my gentle mother thought anything he did was all right—except, maybe, the whisky toddy he would nip each cold morning and leave on the mantle above the fireplace for me to spoon the rock candy.

Taste, smells, sounds and the feel of things are what a boy remembers most. Like the softness of just-hatched baby ducks retrieved from the dewy garden where they had followed their wandering mother down the rows of beans and corn twined in morning-glories.

Or, the freshness of chopped green fodder piped into a silo as three or four boys trotted the small circle packing it down. (We used to get fifty cents a day.)

Sometimes the odor of a skunk victim's pants close to

3

the hot school-room stove would force the teacher at Wartrace to send that boy home. But in summer there was the honeysuckle vine, the couch on the side porch and the scraping of the pan of fudge right off the kitchen stove while reading Ring Lardner's latest "You Know Me, Al" letter, or H. C. Witwer's baseball humor pieces, or Grantland Rice poems, or Horatio Alger or the Rover Boys or the latest baseball guide. Or better still, the afternoon paper. This was close to Paradise.

The going was so easy in Wartrace that people actually did drop in at the barber shop to watch haircuts. But the main diversion was meeting the trains at the railroad depot. There was always a warm greeting to the Sewanee football team traveling to Nashville for its annual Thanksgiving Day game with Vanderbilt. With a branch line to Shelbyville, the depot was a busy place, and clumsy people sometimes dropped coins which rolled between the cracks in the platform and could not be recovered. That is, except by boys who came around at a quieter time with a thin stick that had chewing gum on the end of it.

I've never experienced successive thrills to equal the spotting of a 25-cent piece under the depot platform, its final and delicate extrication after being brought to the top an innumerable number of times, and then the dash to the drugstore to buy a new baseball. This was especially overjoying if the old ball you had been playing with had gone through the stages of busted strings, patched by Mr. Grubbs at the shoe shop with stout, black thread, followed by more wear and tear which finally resulted in removal of the cover and wrapping the ball in black bicycle tape. Boy, it was heavy!

But how beautiful the new ball, stitched in red and blue and so slick that it almost squirted out of the tissue paper. Considered too pretty to hit, everybody usually would agree to a game of catch, first. The smell of a new baseball,

4

the feel of a glove when you ran your fingers 'way up in it and pounded the pocket where a drop or two of machine oil had been rubbed, and then catching the ball with a "give" that prevented stinging—those things never leave you.

There was a baseball diamond in the side lot by our house. Some of my steadiest playmates and warmest childhood friends were Negroes. Two traits of their race most evident then, and now, are: (1) natural rhythm and (2) devotion and responsibility to family and relatives. Have you ever seen a Negro orphanage?

I think Leroy (Satchel) Paige, the everlasting pitcher, as a boy would have fitted right into our bunch. His mother at Mobile once told newspapermen that the family inserted an "i" in their name shortly after Leroy's birth to add a little tone to it, because "Page sounded so much like page in a book." That's worthy of Wartrace when I was a boy. So is the following conversation with Satchel reported by Morris McLemore of the Miami *Daily News* during a 1957 road trip with the Miami baseball club:

"Satch, you've been almost everywhere. Are there any places you've never made that you would like to visit?"

"Just two. Atlantic City and Jerusalem."

"Why is it you've never been to Atlantic City?"

"Never had no contract."

"Why do you want to see Jerusalem?"

"'Cause there's where little baby Jesus was born."

Joe Louis' aptest quotes never surpassed these gems of brilliant simplicity from Satch.

It seems to me that no place could have been more placid than Wartrace prior to World War I. Stanley Horn, the Nashville author and historian, illustrates the serenity of the times with the story of the Middle Tennessee squire rocking on his porch and reading aloud from the just delivered newspaper the news that war had broken out in

5

Europe. "Well," said his hired man, stopping his raking of leaves and looking up at the sky, "I'll say this: they has a mighty nice day for it."

In 1916 the black headlines on the front page weren't nearly as important to me as the sports page accounts of the Nashville Vols' drive to the Southern League pennant. My first sight of a professional baseball park and an introduction to Gabby Street came on the same day—almost too much. Gabby wasn't only the Nashville catcher; he had caught the ball dropped from the Washington Monument. It wasn't until thirty-five years later, in Florida, that I heard the true details of this feat from Street himself.

"It was August 21, 1908," Gabby said. "Walter Johnson was at his peak with Washington and I was looked upon as the only man who could hold this fastest of pitchers. Of course that wasn't true, but I didn't object to the notoriety.

"Pres Gibson, a Washington newspaperman, got the idea that if I could catch Johnson, I could catch anything. He used to argue that way and finally he made a big bet. So I had to help him out.

"We went out to the monument, he with thirteen baseballs and me with a mitt. I don't know why he took thirteen; maybe he was superstitious. Anyhow, he went up to the top and I went out on the grass. The first few balls hit the side of the shaft and never came near me. Then he threw a couple out away from the monument, but I couldn't get to them.

"Then Pres went around to the other side on account of the wind. There were only four times I was close enough to the ball to make a try for the catch. It just happened that the ball I caught was the last one.

"I felt I would get some sort of write-up for it at the time, but I never dreamed this thing would stick with me through life."

In the fall of 1917 a young teacher-coach named Manning Kirby joined the faculty at the Wartrace school. This was to prove a fortunate happenstance for me, though Kirby was there only a few months, volunteering for the Army and heading, ultimately, for France. He was such a favorite that the entire school turned out with all the townspeople to bid him farewell at the station. Ten years later, a few days after I got out of college, Kirby gave me my first job, in Nashville.

We had moved back to Nashville in 1920 and I had entered Duncan Preparatory School. Professor Marvin T. Duncan was noted for his teaching of Latin and the fact that he often gave surprise holidays, on these occasions beginning the chapel exercises in the usual manner with a Biblical reading, then suddenly exclaiming: "And Moses said—we'll have a holiday." His wife was an excellent mathematics and geometry instructor; I found both much more difficult than languages, history or science. One of Duncan's requirements was that a student take penmanship and spelling up to the day he graduated, for which I have been ever grateful.

Looking back, it seems I might have feared over-studying at Duncan. I was highly conscious of the necessity for relaxation. Any afternoon the weather was unfavorable for sports, at the sound of the dismissal bell I would dash for the street car to downtown Nashville, get a gallery seat to Loew's theater for a dime, see all the vaudeville acts, stay through nearly four hours of movies and then see the vaudeville again. At fourteen I knew that Jack Benny honestly could play the violin. Like Bennett Cerf, when I think of the kids of today exposed to so much top-flight talent and super-spectaculars on TV that they're jaded by eight and cruelly critical before they're out of grammar school, I wonder how in the world anybody will be able to amuse them when they grow up.

7

But for my mother, I probably wouldn't have gone to college. She had her heart set on Vanderbilt as far back as the day in 1897 when one of her songs, "The Vanderbilt University Waltz," along with a speech by Chauncey M. Depew, featured the ceremonies at which the statue of Commodore Cornelius Vanderbilt was unveiled. After graduating from Duncan in 1922 I went to work as a soda jerker at the United Cigar Store, hoping to save enough money to enter Vanderbilt. Men like my father who had been traveling salesmen in a small territory were finding it hard to readjust to the changing times. We moved into a bigger house near the university and rented the extra rooms to students.

Prohibition and the liquor traffic developed some tough characters in Nashville in the 1920's and many of them hung out at the United Cigar Store. Ralph McGill, then a Nashville *Banner* reporter and now editor of the Atlanta *Constitution,* named this strip the "Western Front." But at sixteen I was too naive to know much about the gangsterish goings-in, and my best pal around the United was another 16-year-old, name of Phil Harris. Phil's dad conducted the orchestra in the adjacent Knickerbocker Theater, a movie house, and Phil would rush from Hume-Fogg high school to play the drums at the late afternoon and night shows, and spend much of the in-between time at the cigar store. He was just as funny then as he is now, one of the few movie, radio and TV personalities who through the years always has been playing himself. He must be one of the easiest characters for the casting directors and script writers.

Harris as a little boy cut one of his big toes half off chopping wood. He named the toe "Nubbin," and used to talk to it. "Honest, Nubbin, I didn't mean to hit you with that axe," he would say. "Honest I didn't." Phil left Nashville when he was eighteen, but he returns for visits. Playing a round of golf during one of his last trips, he belted his tee shot right down the middle, then remarked walking toward the ball: "You know, since I cured my slice I'm meeting an entirely different class of people out here in the fairway." A sour-mash loyalist, on his next trip Harris wants to place a wreath on the grave of Jack Daniel at Tennessee's only distillery, in Lynchburg (pop. 399), only twenty miles or so from my old hometown Wartrace.

Entering Vanderbilt in 1923, my finest classroom experience was the freshman English course under Dr. Edwin Mims. He aroused one's appreciation for stirring passages of poetry—and for the precisely fitting word. Every freshman memorized Tennyson's *Ulysses,* but I remember best Dr. Mims' zest for Wordsworth's *The Character of the Happy Warrior* and his especial fondness for these lines:

> *". . . Plays, in the many games of life, that one*
> *Where what he most doth value must be won;*
> *Whom neither shape of danger can dismay,*
> *Nor thought of tender happiness betray;*
> *Who not content that former worth stand fast,*
> *Looks forward, persevering to the last,*
> *From well to better, daily self-surpast . . ."*

How Dr. Mims loved that ". . . daily self-surpast"! He pleaded that the liberally educated man should have deep respect for clarity and directness of expression, and that he should "hear, read, mark, learn and inwardly digest."

As a sophomore, I regretted that moving into law school ended the study under Dr. Mims—but it was the only way I could be sure of avoiding chemistry and higher mathematics. ("The study of the fundamentals of mathematics is useful for a sportswriting career," said Chancellor Harvie Barnscomb of Vanderbilt in a witty speech at the 1956 Grantland Rice memorial luncheon given by the Sportsmanship Brotherhood in New York City. "From it, sportswriters learn that when a number of football teams play an equal number of teams on a certain afternoon, only half of them can win. Too, I recommend for sportswriters a study of the classics. A classical education has one great advantage: it is supposed to teach you to ignore those financial rewards which it renders you incapable of earning.")

I think I might even have managed math under the man who is now Vanderbilt's vice-chancellor, Madison Sarratt. He was a young math professor and dean of men then. Today he stands high in NCAA councils by virtue of his sound grasp of how to administer intercollegiate sports. When Sarratt speaks there is honest realism, rare understanding and revealing wit.

Vanderbilt has no journalism course, and even had there been one in my day, I did not then envision a newspaper future. And yet, I always felt I was lucky. So did some other people. The Vanderbilt baseball coach, Josh Cody, a superstitious fellow, thought the team had a better chance to win if I kept custody of the infield practice ball, which I did except on those few and dangerous occasions when I was pitching or playing the infield. And if I showed up at an important basketball game, Josh had a place for me on the bench—always on his left.

As a freshman I had pledged Kappa Sigma fraternity, which at that time had many varsity athletes. Among them was Lynn Bomar, selected All-American end in 1923. Bomar held one of the choice jobs given football players: a street-car "spotter." In this capacity Bomar's duty was to check on whether the conductors rang up all the fares. He was required to fill out a brief report on each street-car ride he made, the conductor's number, the register reading, etc. For each report the Nashville Railway and Light Company paid 25 cents, though limiting his earnings to a maximum of $75 a month. Bomar subcontracted this job to me, and we split $75 every month. I also had the responsibility, as a freshman, of awakening Bomar in time for him to get to classes, and at the end of the school year I did this one morning by rolling the biggest lighted firecracker I ever saw under his bed. When it exploded I feared the whole corner of the fraternity house had been blown off, and I was so scared that even Bomar in his BVD's chasing me across the street and deep into the campus couldn't catch me.

Being in and around sports provided the most fun and happiness I had in college, but it took some time for me to realize that there was a way this could be extended throughout life: by becoming a sportswriter. I was quicker, I think, ascertaining the natural relation between sports and humor and the efficacy of laughter to alleviate tension, in and out of sports.

A baseball teammate and law school classmate was Red Sanders, also a football quarterback, who had an exceptional feel for incongruity. On the morning of an important football game, he might arrange to have posted on the locker room bulletin board a notice that barbecue would be served to the players between halves by the League of Sorority Housemothers. The night before a game, if the Vanderbilt squad of the mid-1920's was seeing a silent movie, Sanders might enter the theater leading me by the hand as I tapped along with a cane. He would find two seats in the most crowded row of strangers and then proceed to read all the sub-titles to his "blind" friend.

Any particularly unctuous, dignified dean or professor might receive a telephone call reported to be from the Eureka Pool Room, saying he had left his cap there the night before and would he pick it up or did he want it sent to him? This type of telephone message was even more satisfying when given to a somewhat shocked secretary when the dean was known to be out of his office.

Sanders had a diabolical urge to upset the precision of others. He would stick little wads of paper inside a friend's hat on a rack to give him a puzzling misfit. When a restaurant waitress wasn't looking, he would print on the menu something like "Special Today—Avocado Stuffed With Minnows," then order it and foment misunderstanding and discord between waitress, chef and the entire kitchen.

The whole idea was that people shouldn't take themselves too seriously and, as the saying goes, a little nonsense now and then is relished by the best of men. Most of the victims would laugh—finally.

We used to, and on occasion still do, engage in a practice which Ted Cox, former Tulane coach, once labeled as "negative bull." It consists of asking a stupid question of a man hepped on a certain subject, then listening to him disdainfully and agitatedly expose your "ignorance." In 1939, Sanders and I were in New Orleans before a spring exhibition between the New York Giants and Cleveland Indians. We met Tom Meany and Garry Schumacher, in my opinion two of New York's best-ever baseball writers, and went to the hotel room of the old American Leaguer, Oscar Vitt, then managing the Indians. After we had visited a little while, Sanders made inquiry as follows:

"Mr. Vitt, was Shoeless Joe Jackson really a good hitter or is all that a lot of bunk?"

"Good hitter!" screamed Vitt, in utter disgust. "Good hitter! He was only the greatest that's ever been! Why . . . . why . . . ."—and then Oscar went to the closet and came out with an umbrella and for twenty minutes favored the unenlightened visitor with a detailed exhibition of Shoeless Joe's batting stance and swing.

It may be deduced that not every single hour of my law school days had been devoted to the mastery of common law pleading, torts, agency, contracts, real property, equity jurisprudence, bills and notes, etc. Indeed, one balmy May afternoon with the breeze in the trees outside the third floor classroom window, I had dozed off during a lecture. For how long, I don't know—perhaps two or three minutes—but I was awakened by the gentle nudge of the classmate seated next to me.

"He called on you," whispered this helpful, protecting friend.

Taken off-guard, flustered, I quickly if desperately responded in loud, clear tones: "I'm not prepared on that case, sir."

The tragedy was that the stern and feared Professor Fitzgerald Hall had not called on anybody. It was an interruption of his lecture that he did not appreciate, and not until years later did I get to explain fully the reason.

The perpetrator of the trick was Sanders, of course. Thirteen years later, he became head football coach at Vanderbilt and upon arrival on the job he seemed over-anxious to impress the university's new chancellor with his seriousness of purpose. It was obvious that Sanders feared the new chancellor might have heard of his undergraduate frivolities. So a dinner was arranged. Everything went splendidly until the time for the coach to drive the chancellor home. In some manner, Sanders' car had sprouted a fox-tail on the radiator cap, and various other swashbuckling accessories. The coach has never revealed to me how he explained that situation successfully to his new boss.

Looking back now, it's a wonder that Manning Kirby, my old teacher at Wartrace, gave me a job in June, 1927, in the legal department of the newly-formed Real Estate Title Company in Nashville, of which he was manager. It was a serious business, examining abstracts, deeds, mortgages, liens, etc., in establishing title to real property. I'll never forget Kirby's friendship. After passing the State bar examination and being licensed to practice law, my problem as the months went by was to decide whether I should and could stay in work so confining and so far removed from sports. Part of the problem was solved in November, 1928, when the company was sold, at a good profit, to the only other title company in Nashville. The other part was that I now had no job.

During the next several weeks I had plenty of time to think, and to reach the definite conclusion that I had to get on a newspaper—somehow. That's the only thing I wanted.

Kirby arranged for me to see Jimmy Stahlman of the *Banner*. He gave me a choice: an opening on the classified ad desk at $25 a week or a cub reporter at $6 a week. I jumped at the reporting job.

This was June, 1929. Ralph McGill had just left as sports editor to join the Atlanta *Constitution*. Ralph Perry, a veteran political writer, was filling in as sports editor. I spent the first few weeks on the police beat, then was assigned to Vanderbilt football. The next year I became sports editor.

I believe in luck. If you think you're lucky, you are. I was lucky not just to get the chance to work at what I liked; I was luckier in the fact that Jimmy Stahlman, owner and publisher of the *Banner*, and E. B. Stahlman, Jr., executive vice-president, both came up through the editorial department of the paper, both competed in sports (Jimmy for years held the Southern intercollegiate low hurdles record), both at one time wrote sports and both retain a lively interest in sports.

I have no idea as to what is the best preparation for the sportswriting life. It has been described as requiring "a realist with a laugh who takes his job seriously, but not himself."

14

Or maybe lots of men get into sportswriting because they are "humanists." A "humanist" has been defined as "a person who can't do anything with his hands."

I still have trouble with typewriter ribbons.

Some Of The Gold Rubbed Off

The 1920's were felicitous times for the world, fabulous times for sports and fortunate times for sportswriters.

Never before or since have there been so many heroic-size figures in so many different fields of athletic endeavor. It was the crowded era of Babe Ruth in baseball, Jack Dempsey in boxing, Bobby Jones in golf, Bill Tilden in tennis and Red Grange, along with Knute Rockne and his Four Horsemen of Notre Dame, in football. And many, many other first-magnitude stars. Any boy going through high school and college in this Golden Age of Sport felt the impact of their dazzling performances and responded to their colorful personalities. I gladly attest that some of the gold rubbed off on me. Unconsciously, I must have been conditioned to some extent for sportswriting as a vocation.

There were writers then who were just as gifted in their work as the athletes were in their play, and I read every line I could find by Grantland Rice, Ring Lardner, Westbrook Pegler, Damon Runyon, H. G. Salsinger, John Kieran, W. O. McGeehan, Paul Gallico, Bill Cunningham, Ed Danforth, Ralph McGill, Morgan Blake, Blinkey Horn and other top-notchers of the sports section.

There was a young Associated Press sports editor, Alan Gould, whose lead paragraphs on the national spectacles were paragons of clarity and comprehensiveness. And the hole-by-hole, stroke-by-stroke account by the eccentric Davis J. Walsh of International News Service dictated from the Interlachen golf course at Minneapolis in 1930 when Bob Jones was winning the U.S. Open championship for the third leg on his Grand Slam was the most brilliant spot coverage I've known in sports.

It was Kerr N. Petrie of the New York *Herald Tribune* who wrote, after one of Jones' superb rounds: "They wound up the Mechanical Man of Golf and sent him clicking around the course today." And when Bob (he never liked "Bobby") completed the Grand Slam by capturing the U.S. Amateur at Merion, Pa., George Trevor of the *Sun* concluded eloquently: "He has entrenched his record safely and forever within the Impregnable Quadrilateral of Golf."

Jones' Grand Slam and Babe Ruth's lifetime home run total of 714 are generally regarded as the top individual sports achievements of all time. However, Jones' feat of finishing first or second in the U.S. and British Open championships eleven of twelve times between 1922 and 1930 could easily be greater. But my purpose isn't to recount or compare the extraordinary accomplishments of the Golden Age; rather, it's to submit the opinion that several of the most glittering stars of the Golden Age are heroes still because of 24-carat qualities of character.

Consider the fact that it was a generation ago that Jones and Dempsey and Grange and Ruth reigned their realms of sport. Yet call those names now and anyone with the mildest bent for sports will respond instantaneously and knowingly. Such was and is their magnetism that they have stayed at the top of the hit parade through the years, and admiration for them still grows.

"Babe Ruth was my favorite sports guy," Joe Williams

of the New York *World-Telegram* commented not long ago. "The Bam had the precious gift of being himself at all times. He rolled through a long and gripping career, almost constantly in the glare of the white lights, and at the finish he was essentially the same gangling kid . . . unchanged and unspoiled."

The enduring appeal of Dempsey, Jones and Grange is traceable to their humility and graciousness. I came to know them well. Each was as friendly and available to sportswriters in Nashville or Indianapolis or Des Moines as to those in New York, Chicago or Los Angeles.

No newspaperman ever wrote as much about one individual as the late O. B. Keeler of the Atlanta *Journal* did about Bob Jones while he became a living legend. I knew Jones only slightly when he was winning his golf championships, but I know that as a man he has continued shining with an aureate magnificence. Being a world celebrity only made him bigger as a human being. Jones, Grange and Dempsey were together in Nashville for a day and night in September, 1953. Also on hand was Bill Corum, comfortable, perceptive columnist of the New York *Journal-American,* who described a luncheon scene:

"Red Grange, a still slim and racy-looking man with dark auburn hair, thinning a little now, moved into the big room. Once he was as close to a darting, spinning shaft of light across the crossbars of a football field as any man has been before or since. . . . Now it was the big fellow, Jack Dempsey. There's something about that Dempsey, forever boyish. . . . Through the archway came a man walking slowly with a cane. A proud man in the way that a man should be proud in the face of whatever may befall him. Suddenly every man in the room was on his feet. Hand clapping drew as close to a cheer as the clapping of hands can come. Tears jumped to sting a little behind your eyes. Bobby Jones smiled. 'Thank you, gentlemen,' he said. And then, turning the moment deftly, as the champions and those who are born with such a knack can do, he said: 'But I know why you are applauding. I'm the only man in the room who had the foresight to bring his highball with him from the bar.' It was a fine thing, a very fine thing. Not many men, whatever they may have done, ever got a tribute so truly spontaneous and touching."

In the warmth of Bob Jones' gentle nature, others were scarcely conscious of his affliction, a spinal paralysis.

Even in Bob's sense of humor, always there was a certain softness. He had been intrigued by the veteran caddies at St. Andrews, Scotland, when he won the British Amateur in 1930. "In experience, wisdom and dignity, they're in a group to themselves," he once told me. "There was one, perhaps seventy, carrying the clubs of an unpleasant fellow who was playing very poor golf and blaming it all on the caddy. The old caddy maintained a dignified silence, of course—until his man finally declared, addressing the other members of the match: 'For this round, I believe I've drawn the worst caddy in the world!'

" 'Oh, no, sir,' said the caddy. 'That would be quite too great a coincidence.' "

In today's newspapers the heroes of the Golden Age are referred to oftener than the more recent sports stars of the 1930's and 1940's, and I wouldn't be surprised if the same thing is true twenty and thirty years from now. Their names carry a hand-me-down lustre.

One night before a scheduled heavyweight title defense by Joe Louis in New York, I was eating dinner with other sportswriters. The table conversation soon got around to Jack Dempsey—and stayed there. Weather postponed the fight the next night, and the next, and in two more dinner sessions at Toots Shor's the talk always got around to Dempsey, somehow. I remember a stocky, dark man named

Charlie Murray, telling about the first time he ever heard of Dempsey, and of bringing him East for the first time.

"I scarcely knew his name when I did it," Murray said. "I was promoting fights in Buffalo. Fireman Jim Flynn was to fight Carl Morris for me on this certain Monday night in what shaped up as my best attraction in years. But this Flynn, he up and calls me Wednesday and says he's going out to Peoria for a fight Friday night and will be back to Buffalo Sunday for the Morris fight.

"I said that he couldn't do that to me and I raised hell about it, but he told me not to worry, that it was nothing more than a workout, that he was fighting a punk named Dempsey and would knock him out in the first round.

"Well, Dempsey knocks Flynn out in the first round. When I heard the news that night, I couldn't believe it, so I telephoned a sports editor I knew in Chicago to find out if it was true. He said it wasn't only true, but that it was no fluke, and this kid Dempsey must have the goods.

"I found out that Jack Kearns was managing Dempsey, I offered him $750 and expenses to bring Dempsey to Buffalo to fight Morris, he accepted, I set the bout back a week and wondered what was gonna' happen.

"When they showed up and I saw Dempsey, I was burned up. He weighed about 175, maybe 180 at the most. Morris weighed 260. I told them the fight was off. I wasn't going to ruin myself with a joke match. But Kearns and then Dempsey put up an argument, and this kid convinced me. He said that if he didn't knock Morris out, he wouldn't take a penny. We didn't make any deal like that, of course, but I went on with the fight.

"With the opening bell this Dempsey leaps into Morris like a panther and cuts him up so that they have to stop the fight in the fourth round."

It was the same kind of butchery, reducing 245-pound

Jess Willard to a shapeless mass, that brought 187-pound Dempsey the championship and electrified the sports world. Boxing experts agreed that Dempsey was the deadliest killer outside the jungle. James P. Dawson of the New York *Times* wrote: "This bobbing, weaving tiger has the savage instinct to tear into and rip and slash his opponent into instant helplessness, with contempt for the consequences."

Yet, outside the ring, Dempsey was courteous, considerate, gentle, with an indefinable charm that still makes him a traffic-stopper. He was sixty before he confessed that he had been a mom's boy. "I never was a hobo," he said. "Sure, I rode the freight trains some; out in Utah when I was a kid, nearly everybody did. But to be honest with you, I never stayed away from home long because I missed my mother too much. Maybe I shouldn't be telling this, but as the next to youngest of eleven kids, I used to help her with the washing and the cooking."

This very definite but little known tenderness was reflected in Dempsey's attentiveness, love and devotion in the rearing of his two daughters.

A sportswriter's good times were enriched if he knew Red Grange. I've known him a long time, and each January for the past several years I've been with him at the Senior Bowl game. Like Jones and Dempsey, he has that certain "plus" quality that glows.

I marvel and re-marvel at the modesty which makes Grange sidestep adroitly any attempted conversational replay of his four touchdowns in twelve minutes for Illinois against Michigan in 1924, and his scoring runs of 60, 55 and 15 yards in the mud against a dumbfounded 1925 University of Pennsylvania team, rated the mightiest in the East. "Grange is melody, and symphony, and crashing sound," wrote Damon Runyon. "He is poetry. He is brute force. He is the doggondest football player I ever saw. He is Jack Dempsey, Babe Ruth, Al Jolson, Paavo Nurmi and Man o' War all rolled into one."

Named All-American as a sophomore, again as a junior and again as a senior, for his running, Red's greatest thrill in college and pro football was:

"In 1923, when we played Iowa, the defending Big Ten champion, Iowa had beaten Purdue and Ohio State and was unscored-on. Going into the fourth quarter, they led us, 6 to 0. We got a touchdown on desperate passes, but missed the extra point, and the score was 6 to 6. With a minute to play, we had the ball on the 50-yard line and it was decided to try a field goal. I held the ball for Earl Britton. It was snapped from center, I put it down and he gave it a powerful leg stroke. I kneeled there, sorta' praying. It went through."

Illinois was not scored on again that year.

When Grange turned professional, he was the lure that pulled 73,000 into the Polo Grounds. But in his thought processes he never has had the individualistic approach. When I asked him to name the best all-round football player he ever saw, Red said:

"Bronko Nagurski, as a fullback or tackle. At 238 pounds and six feet, three inches, he was all muscle. He was the fastest big football player I ever saw, and the most powerful. There never has been a stronger ball-carrier, one as sure to gain a few yards every try, and he was also a fine short passer. But with all his physical assets, his natural ability, he also was a splendid team man. He was never thinking of himself. So often you see little fellows, or players lacking in ability, who are great team men, who have wonderful dispositions. And we say: 'Isn't it a shame that they aren't bigger, or that they don't have more skill?' Well, Nagurski had everything. And he never was injured. One

22

time I asked Bronk if he had ever been hurt. He said he had a black eye once."

Nagurski and the Galloping Ghost—what a pair!

When I came into sportswriting, Knute Rockne of Notre Dame was the king of the coaches, the most dynamic and possessed with the best feel for the crowd. He was also the foremost personal salesman, and if you think Frank Leahy twenty years later was adept at lulling an opponent, listen to Rockne's sweet talk to a reporter from the *Daily Princetonian* on the eve of the 1923 Notre Dame-Princeton game:

"While we do not expect that our little university can win a game against so powerful a team as Princeton, we do think this opportunity to come to this Revolutionary site and to see the great University will be a benefit to us. I believe firmly that our boys will get a good deal out of their contacts with Princeton men."

They did, twenty-five points to Princeton's two.

Rockne was the first coach, as far as I know, who insisted that his players entering the coaching field acquire the ability to speak in public. Many people think that he also equipped each man with a set of jokes, but it's just that Rockne's humor rubbed off on them.

Had Rockne not been killed in an airplane crash March 31, 1931, the entire present concept of football might be different, for he was inventive, enterprising and a step ahead of many rivals.

Not even Jones, Dempsey, Ruth or Grange completely dominated his field of sport as did Bill Tilden, who ruled tennis for six consecutive years in the 1920's. Much later, the last time I saw him in action, Tilden was fifty-two or fifty-three, he had played in more than 10,000 matches and was still going strong in a game that places extreme strain on the legs. He was one of the most remarkable athletes of all time.

Tilden was also a shrewd showman if at times a "ham" actor. He impressed me as a forerunner of present-day "villains" in professional wrestling; always an overwhelming favorite and disliked by the audience, he would put himself in the hole by losing a few games to an opponent as the crowd envisioned a savory upset. Then, when he considered this had gone far enough, Tilden would blow their "hero" off the court.

That such a brilliant career should have terminated in shame was one of the saddest tragedies in American sports. What struck me as inexcusably cruel was the handling of his case and his virtual abandonment by his acquaintances. I realize that Tilden had few friends.

But here was an individual who, while he was winning tennis glory for the United States, was acceptable despite wide knowledge of his aberrations brought on by Nature's having dealt him a sorry hand. Then when he became involved in serious difficulties, ill and probably in need of quarantine, he was sentenced to the county road.

What made Tilden great? His concentration, possibly. I once heard him say: "Tennis calls for more concentration than any sport. In golf you play the game stroke by stroke. You know where your tee shot should go, and then there's the green. But in tennis you have to map out your tactics or strategy several strokes ahead. You work to get your opponent into a certain spot where he can't make a return. This play calls for many strokes, here and there. In tennis you have extended concentration. In golf and baseball and other sports, it usually is for only the next play. And in tennis, unlike baseball and football, you are all alone."

Tilden was a master of timing, which is the foundation

of everything we do well. He had inconceivable coordination of mind and muscle.

Incidentally, I think tennis and billiards run truest to form of any sports. The incomparable Willie Hoppe offered good proof of this in billiards, and tennis will be even more formful when—and if—a uniform playing surface, probably concrete, is adopted throughout the world.

There were other transcendent performers in the 1920's. Even the majestic Man o' War, "de mostest hoss," running like a leaping flame while his red coat gleamed, fitted the grandeur of the Golden Age. As did Earl Sande. And Tommy Hitchcock and Devereux Milburn in polo, and Johnny Weissmuller and Gertrude Ederle in swimming, and of course Charley Paddock and Paavo Nurmi in track.

Nurmi shattered every distance mark in the books, knocking two whole seconds off the world record for the mile. This seemed to excite lots of people, except the college professor who was irked by his students' interest in the matter and who, attempting disparagement, asked: "And how, please tell me, does this distinguished Finnish gentleman propose to employ the time he has saved?"

Nurmi's mile and most of the other individual feats have been surpassed, and very probably they all will be in time. But that will not diminish the Golden Age and the big thing that was accomplished. The essence of the athletes who glittered in the Golden Age was crowd appeal. They made all America sports conscious. They gave new dimensions to sportswriting and sportswriters by giving us an audience of ever-increasing millions.

The Toy Department

I'm not sure who created the term "toy department" for the sports staff of a newspaper. I think it was Westbrook Pegler. I do know it fitted the space and the occupants thereof on the *Banner* during my first years there. Still does, I hope.

The editorial department was on the third floor of the newspaper plant at Third Avenue and Commerce Street in Nashville. Our little portion of it consisted of four desks backed up against each other on the edge of the city room. It could be identified by the layers of schedules, sports pictures, telephone numbers and other allegedly useful information pasted haphazardly on the wall.

I can remember one afternoon in 1932 when we were advised that a class from George Peabody Teachers College was touring the building. When they reached the sports department, two of us were on the floor playing marbles— for keeps—while our tallest staffer was shooting a basketball at the Western Union clock on the wall. It wasn't quite as bad as it may sound; the clock had been giving trouble and the paper was sponsoring a marble tournament with which somebody, as a refresher, had to become familiar.

In those days nothing seemed to matter much just as long as the newspaper got out, and everybody had fun getting it out. There was a lot of pride in the work—and a lot of play. It was a robust, unpredictable place. Publishing week-day afternoons and Sunday morning, we got to work no later than 7 A.M., and it was no shock occasionally to find some weary associate stretched across the copy desk asleep. Most likely he had stayed in the card game in the photographic department so late that it wasn't worth going home.

On Saturdays we worked straight through from seven in the morning to two o'clock Sunday morning. A late Saturday night pastime was to shoot a .22 rifle at the rats that scampered about on the overhead heating pipes near the dimly-lit entrance to the city room. This often proved an unnerving greeting to unexpected visitors just stepping off the elevator.

Whenever a reporter or desk man was missing, the first place to be checked was the speakeasy around the corner. One Saturday night a prodigal returned from there with an odd grievance, a pound of butter and a knife. He smeared the keyboards of four typewriters before being disarmed and dismissed.

The managing editor, a tall, spry man whose red hair was growing white, had an inflexible voice that matched his name, Marmaduke B. Morton. He smoked a cob pipe and he was a good newspaperman. By the time I came along, Mr. Morton was turning over most of the active duties to his assistant, Howard Eskridge, a milder-mannered man who would have looked undressed without a cigar in his mouth, and it didn't make much difference to him whether it stayed lighted or went out. Those were the days when many men partook of the luxury of barber shop

27

shaves and Eskridge was one of the steadiest patrons of a shop across the street until the barber, finishing up on him one day, pointed to a set of false teeth on the shelf which he explained an earlier customer had left after, apparently, taking the barber's by mistake.

One of the veteran *Banner* copy editors had never succumbed to the use of pencil or typewriter in writing heads. He stuck with his pen and inkwell. Each afternoon, at precisely five minutes before the deadline for the city edition, he would leave his chair and go into the wire room to check the teletype machines for any late news. Dry ice was a new-fangled thing in those days and the boy who sold Eskimo pies through the building always had a spare particle which invariably found its way into the copy editor's inkwell, and each afternoon shortly after his return to his station, it would bubble high and beautifully. The nice old gentleman would sit there and stare at it, mystified.

A younger man on the news desk, most meticulous, always kept a dozen freshly sharpened pencils and an assortment of straight-stemmed pipes in his drawer along with a can of his favorite brand of blended smoking tobacco. The latter would become a bit more of a mixture when, in his absence, the office boy added a dash of pencil shavings.

The late James H. Street was a lively character in the cast around the *Banner* in 1929. He was head of the Associated Press bureau, gathering the material then for the successful novels he was to write, but I remember him best for the sermons he could deliver on any subject, fire-and-brimstone style. He had been a boy evangelist in Mississippi.

The brightest *Banner* star, a true genius, was Joe Parrish, now the world-known cartoonist of the Chicago *Tribune*. Joe came to the *Banner* straight out of high school at Dickson, forty miles away, and never took a drawing lesson in his life. His political cartoons of the heated Tennessee gubernatorial campaigns of the day are collector's items. Parrish also did a cartoon for our "stand-through" sports page every Sunday.

Francis Robinson, assistant general manager of the Metropolitan Opera Association, was on the *Banner* staff as a reporter in the 1930's. His many talents included the art of imitating the voices of well-known Nashville people, notably Chancellor James H. Kirkland of Vanderbilt, and Robinson was on the other end of the telephone from many a person who's still puzzled. Incidentally, Francis still carries with him the not altogether revealing headline written by a hurried, harried *Banner* desk man on a story telling of five people being killed when an automobile went over a bluff: "LOOKS OUT AS CAR GOES OVER."

If I seem to overemphasize the zany aspects of journalism in the late 1920's and early 1930's, it's because those things are the easiest remembered. And they were not peculiar to the *Banner;* generally, there was less conformity and habituated routine, more effervescence and sentiment and individuality. If there was a little fun, there was also a lot of forcefulness.

The *Banner* reflected the personality of Jimmy Stahlman, who had been route boy, campus correspondent, reporter, sports writer, city editor and editorial director—and had been designated by his grandfather, Major E. B. Stahlman, a most formidable man, to assume control of the newspaper, which he did at the Major's death in 1930. Jimmy Stahlman set the editorial pace with his own dynamic qualities—spirit, drive, boldness and decision. He never hedged; he was willing to stand up and be counted. And could he get mad! Sometimes the windows rattled when he stormed from his office into the city room. He kept everybody on the ball. Yet I've never known a man who more enjoyed a funny story, or more liked to pull a gag or—in the clutch—was surer to be compassionate. Now sixty-four, he's so strong of mind and will that he has made himself into the epitome of composure, the most brilliant example of fire-control I've seen. Looks like he's fifty.

My clearest memory of Stahlman's enthusiasm for getting a story recalls the kidnaping of Mrs. Alice Speed Stoll, of Louisville, Kentucky, by Thomas H. Robinson, Jr., of Nashville, who obtained $50,000 in ransom money and was a fugitive for nineteen months before being captured by the FBI at Glendale, California.

I had known Robinson in college. When he was flown back to Louisville for trial, I suggested to Stahlman that there might be a chance of getting to see him and finding out how and where he had spent those nineteen months. He was all for it. I drove to Louisville with Robinson's father, "retained" as one of his attorneys in the hope that this might enable me to see Tom. The scheme not only didn't work, because the opposition newspaper got wise to it, but on our arrival at the Federal building in Louisville the U. S. marshal and his deputies were so inhospitable as to not even let me in the court clerk's office.

Robinson's trial was set for five o'clock that afternoon. He pleaded guilty and was sentenced so quickly—all within less than two minutes—that everybody was taken by surprise and the whole place was in confusion. As Robinson was led back to jail, I fell in with his mother, father and other relatives, just to see how far I might get without being stopped. I got all the way, right into his cell.

Tom told me the highlights of his hiding-out as Public Enemy No. 1, his narrow escapes and what led up to his capture. He also gave me the name of a girl who had been with him for more than a year, and a clue as to how she might be found.

When the FBI discovered I was in the cell, I was hustled out promptly and not tenderly. The FBI man said I positively could not make use of any information I had obtained from Robinson.

"What if I should?" I asked.

"You would be barred forever from practicing law in Kentucky!" he said.

A deplorable fate, thought I, but the story had to be used. And Stahlman demanded: "Let's find the girl."

He went with me to New York on that mission. She proved to be a story as writeable as the first series.

I've found, in and out of sports, that the stories which seem cinches often fall flat, while the one-chance-in-a-hundred longshots sometimes materialize when you least expect it. And another's enthusiasm can keep you trying when otherwise you'd quit.

Our sports staff back in 1929 and the early 1930's consisted of three regulars and a part-time golf writer. The market editor, R. A. Wilson, also wrote a weekly fishing and hunting column, and another elderly man, John C. Cooke, who covered the Federal building as his regular beat, doubled as turf editor under the nom de plume, Jay See See. As a rookie I was fortunate to break in under a man like Ralph Perry who tried to implant in each member of his staff a sense of typography and make-up as well as writing. At this time the *Banner's* city editor was Charlie Moss, now its executive editor. Moss taught me plenty, mainly that if you believe a man can handle an assignment or a job, leave him alone. Turn it over to him and don't bother him; let him do it his way. If he can't do it, get somebody else. But as long as the man is delivering for you, don't be looking over his shoulder all the time and pestering him with your suggestions. Let him develop his own initiative and responsibility—and confidence.

Then and now, that's the best newspaper advice I've heard. And I'm sure it works as well in any other business.

Through 1931 and 1932, the Depression drained very little of the lightheartedness out of sportswriting. We were getting part of our salary in scrip, which was to be taken to the grocery store and exchanged for victuals. And were we glad to get it!

The Greek restaurant on the corner opposite the paper, named the "Banner Cafe," extended credit from payday to payday, writing the amount of meal purchases "on the wall."

Nobody minded work. There were 70-hour weeks, more often 80. I can remember driving to Knoxville to cover a University of Tennessee football game, filing a brief bulletin lead for the bulldog edition, then racing back to Nashville to write the story, thus saving the telegraph toll. And I found ONE man, Bob McGaw, putting out our Sunday sports section all by himself. The *other* sportswriter was anesthetized and absent. The modern ten-man staff hardly knows the meaning of emergency.

Our staffers did mighty little traveling during those lean years. When we did, our expense report underwent X-ray scrutiny. One day I gave the acting state news editor a near coronary by faking a collect long distance telephone call from Phoenix, Arizona, from one of his rural correspondents who had arranged a free bus trip to the West and was air-mailing her stories. Even Gene Fowler would have been taxed to outwit our auditors. It was Fowler who, on a newspaper assignment to the Far North many years ago, found himself several hundred dollars short due to the cost of inside straights and anti-freeze compound. He padded every item, still was shy, so added a notation that the lead dog on the sled team had succumbed to the rigors of the journey, and wrote in $100 recompense for the noble beast's owner. Then he dashed off the additional expenditure: "Flowers for bereaved bitch, $50."

As big league baseball clubs came through Nashville to play exhibition games, I began to wonder if the best job in the world wasn't that of baseball writer in New York or

Chicago or any major league city—on a morning newspaper. All that Charlie Segar and Richards Vidmer and Jim Dawson had to do, seemed like, was to get to the ball park 30 or 45 minutes before the afternoon game, pick up a few notes on the field, write those notes during the game, afterward spend no more than half an hour writing the game story, then they were through work until the next afternoon. This *was* a choice assignment until night baseball turned it into a nightmare for the morning paper writers; now they have to rush new leads for each edition and write the game story each night at breakneck speed. And the irregular hours of night and day baseball make the job almost as tough for the afternoon newspapermen.

Even in 1932, though, I feared that a baseball writing job, with all the travel involved, was more suited to an unmarried man. I wasn't married, but I had notions. A notion, rather. Her name was Kay Early, of Nashville.

I had been a friend of her older brother, John Early, Jr., and the first time I remember seeing Kay she was about fourteen, in pigtails and riding her pony, and I was eighteen and a Vanderbilt sophomore, and there's no age gap as wide, I think, as between an 18-year-old boy and a 14-year-old girl.

Occasionally I would eat Sunday dinner at the Early home. It was an old family place on the edge of Nashville, originally just a summer home, with the Indian name "Pontotoc." There were a tennis court, orchard, baseball diamond, pastures full of ponies and stables of horses. Mr. Early, the grandson of a Methodist bishop, was a stern man, the chairman of the county school board and the type called "Father" by his children. He cracked the whip in more ways than one. Driving a horse and buggy to town every day, he was probably the last man in Nashville to give in to the automobile. He was a breeder of horses, an authority on trotters and pacers, and his fondness for them accounted for his business: a saddle and harness dealer. He was one of the founders of the Tennessee State Fair and always was the official starter for the races there. The champion pacer, John R. Gentry, owned by E. H. Harriman of New York City, was retired to the Early place and died there. Mrs. Early wasn't a horse enthusiast, caring more for music and writing and the rearing of three daughters and two sons.

After John Early, Jr., left college to work for Standard Oil in Java and Sumatra, I don't remember seeing Kay again for five or six years. I did notice in the newspapers that she had made the All-State basketball team as a side center on the championship Peabody Demonstration School team. Other times, I read about her winning blue ribbons at horse shows. In 1931, she was back from teaching riding at Mount Ida School near Boston and John was home from the Far East on a leave, and she chanced to drive us to the train to accompany the Vanderbilt football team on a trip to Atlanta for the Georgia Tech game. From that moment I knew she was the one. I think that's something you find out in the eyes, though I wouldn't attempt to explain further.

A woman marrying a newspaperman deserves to know what she's getting into—the odd hours, the sudden changes in plans, the necessity for adaptability. Some like it, some don't. She did. But she had to prove it to herself by accompanying me to sports events and waiting, waiting, waiting afterward, while I had to work. She even pretended she didn't mind when we had to leave wherever we were so I could get to Radio Station WSM at 10:30 every night, Monday through Friday, for a sports program I had.

In courting Kay for two years, I don't think I would have made as many trips to Camp Riva-Lake at Winchester, Tennessee, where she was a summer counselor, had I known the trips would be repeated for eternity. Our four daughters all have gone there, and I am known by every leaf and rock on the place.

We were married on November 2, 1933. I was twenty-seven. My birthday was on the 27th of August and my college class was '27. But I've never won on the number at roulette, or collected any 2-7 daily double or quinella tickets.

Frequently, from the start, I brought sports people to our home with little or no notice, but with ease and confidence because of Kay's adjustable nature as a hostess. She even does the carving now at the dinner table. I did it the first ten years but quit abruptly on a Christmas Day when the turkey turned out to be a Tartar because the new cook didn't know how to work the stove. All brothers and sisters and their families eat Christmas dinner with us, as does Mrs. Early, the only grandparent now living. I knew I couldn't carve that turkey and serve all those plates and get to the New Year's Day bowl game in time for the kickoff.

We've lived in the same place since 1938; it's fifteen minutes from the office but country enough for ponies and stable and basketball court. Each Christmas Eve afternoon the stable is turned into a Bethlehem manger scene with neighborhood children in the Nativity roles. This has been going on for so many years that last Christmas one of the littlest angels of 1940 was now portraying Mary. The neighborhood dogs are cast as sheep, and their occasional barking isn't nearly so disrupting as to have the Three Wise Men arriving late for the show on motorbikes, their costumes (bathrobes and head scarfs) flowing in the breeze.

I've been home every Christmas but two, both those at the Rose Bowl. I think Christmas glows with an unbeatable color combination: green of a tree, orange of a wood-burning fire and pink of a happy child's cheeks.

35

I suppose one of the severest tests of a child's disposition comes to a fourth daughter who's the last to get hand-me-down clothes. Last Christmas our littlest, Carolyn, 10, got a red skirt which had been worn by her sisters Kay, 22; Ellen, 19; and Lee, 15. For Valentine's Day, her mother re-designed it into a heart motif, and Carolyn wore it to school. When I came home that afternoon, no one was there, but the skirt was pinned to the bed in our room along with a piece of paper on which was scrawled, in pencil: "CHANGE TO BUNNY."

In November, 1937, the *Banner* and The Nashville *Tennessean*, its morning rival, formed the Newspaper Printing Corporation to produce both papers. The *Tennessean* discontinued its evening editions and the *Banner* dropped its Sunday edition. Both papers retained their separate editorial identities and moved into a new plant with separate editorial offices. If anything, the news-getting competition was keener than ever.

It was nice for us on the *Banner* not to have to work those long Saturdays. But with only a six-day afternoon paper it meant a new approach to the coverage of sports. Now, more than ever, the accent was on features rather than straight news stories. Duties were divided more sharply; one man would specialize in a particular sport. I think a by-line is more important on a sports story than on a news story. A story on a flood or fire or wreck doesn't have to be written by a man who knows all about such things. A man who has reported forty floods or fires or wrecks has little advantage over the man who has covered none, whereas the sportswriter who has covered forty ball games, particularly if following the same team, establishes authenticity in his writing.

But I think statistics have a permanent value even in

sports sections with the most extreme p.m. angle. Opinions die, but records live, it's said, and readers like some information they can nail down. We carry in agate type—it takes no more than an inch and a half column space—a condensation of how the runs were scored in Nashville's Southern Association ball games, even if such facts are eighteen hours old. Nothing popularized a sport as much as the box score did baseball. Basketball summaries are including more and more exact information, but the story of a football game just can't seem to be told in figures.

Within my time, fastest-developing and most beneficial adjuncts to sports staffs are the college athletic information directors. They render invaluable service. College presidents such as Dr. Rufus Harris of Tulane recognize that football is a school's prime area of public relations; Tulane's specialist in this field, Horace Renegar, holds a high administrative post. Incidentally, when I covered the Vanderbilt-Ohio State football game in 1933, the Ohio State athletic publicist was James B. (Scotty) Reston, now the distinguished New York *Times*man.

In our toy department at the *Banner*, high school sports get a tremendous play. I think it's the best investment in citizenship a newspaper can make. Many boys can be reached best through sport, some only through sport. Yet I would not pretend that it is a wholly altruistic utility. There are twenty-three teams in Nashville and thrice that number in the area; when a boy is playing on a team, his parents and relatives and neighbors are interested, and thus potential subscribers. Moreover, if a boy of high school age starts reading the paper, he's likely to stay with you through life. We print the full name of each starting player in every high school game lineup. Selection of weekly all-star teams is one of many built-in features of the year-round program, which is climaxed by a Banquet of Champions bringing together the high school winners with the college "Coach of the Year" and "Player of the Year" in the Southeastern Conference. What can make a sportswriter's good life even better is his newspaper's active indorsement of and intense working interest in such projects; E. B. Stahlman, Jr., personally supervises this one.

The best sports editor I've known was Stanley Woodward when he operated at the New York *Herald Tribune*. I say that despite observing him in a shin-kicking contest with any and all comers at Bear Mountain Inn near West Point on the night before an Army-Notre Dame game. I subscribe to Woodward's dictum:

"The most effective way to run a sports department is to deal yourself out of it as fast as you can. You should get it organized so that it will run by itself for six months at a time if necessary. If you can accomplish this, then you yourself will be free to cover such assignments as are naturally yours and to take up the things that go wrong, night or day, without being hampered by routine work. You also will have leisure to devise improvements in the conduct of the department and to figure out ideas for stories and features."

I believe a sports staff functions at its happiest and most efficiency if each member gets to star at some time. There's where the changing seasons are so serviceable, and variety so unmotived. I've been convinced for a long time that one of the manifest, contagious appeals of Lawrence Welk's orchestra is that each artist gets to shine individually.

However, writers these days derive less and less psychic income from seeing their by-lines. Salary, understandably, is more important. Money may not be everything, but it will help until everything comes along.

Stability is a prize asset to a staff, with its increment of local knowledge. Of ten *Banner* sportswriters—George Leonard, Dudley Green, Edgar Allen, Bill Roberts, Bob Witt,

John Steen, John DuVal, Lee Callaway, Ed Given and Foster Anderson—five have been there 23, 16, 15, 12 and 10 years.

Actually, nobody can teach another person how to write. But if I reduced to simplest terms the things I think sportswriters strive for most, they would be:

Accuracy, speed and sparkle.

Beyond those, he's blessed if he has originality and a sense of the dramatic.

It's easy for a sportswriter to attract attention if he regularly lambasts somebody, or is sarcastically critical. It's more difficult to be fair, and still be readable. One of the best approaches to fairness is to ask one's self questions similar to the ones confronting the official scorer in baseball:

If I'm the hitter, do I think I deserve credit for a hit?

If I'm the fielder, do I think I deserve an error?

If I'm the pitcher, how do I think it should be scored?

What's the fairest thing for all three?

Football Will Never Be The Same

The fascination and joy of sports, and the grip it can get on a person, showed plainly in the career of Dan McGugin, football coach at Vanderbilt (1904-34). Fresh from the University of Michigan, he developed sensational teams from the start, reigned supreme in the South for many years and won glorious intersectional victories. Meanwhile—long before his retirement from coaching—McGugin had become a successful, busy attorney with many interests. Yet to him, always the game was the thing, and the people in and around it.

A man didn't have to play football under McGugin to get to know him well, or to comprehend—and admire—his coaching philosophy. To him, teams were men, not machines. He was hearty, convivial, with big, kindly Irish eyes of blue, and an infinite deal of wit. My association with him, dating from days in college, might be likened to that of the World War II airborne division officer who discovered that one fellow in the plane had not obeyed his orders to jump, and said: "If you aren't a paratrooper, why are you here?" And the boy said: "I just like to be around para-troopers." I was around McGugin and Vanderbilt football players a lot.

While McGugin had brought new techniques to Southern football, and was a clever strategist, his foremost quality was the ability to inspire men. Not as a staccato fire-eater, like Knute Rockne; Dan spoke softly and slowly. He was a master of psychology, keying a team with an almost-sacred approach, or breaking tension with some hilarious prank or remark.

Most coaches of today say that their players would laugh at them if they attempted to fire their emotions. "Besides," one told me recently, "I want my players to go on the field clear-eyed and able to see, not crying." To each his own, but I saw a teary Vanderbilt team take the field against highly-favored Minnesota and score a ringing upset after these quietly-spoken words from McGugin:

"With each one of you boys there was a time—you knew nothing about it, of course—a time when you were two months old, or five months, when your mother looked at you in the cradle, and she wondered, she asked herself, what kind of heart beat in that little body; of how this boy, as he grew into a man, would meet his first real test of courage; whether, when that time came, if she could feel the pride that only a mother can feel for a son who is courageous . . . and fearless . . . or whether there might, perhaps, have to be a different feeling. She knew that such a time, such a day, would come. Today . . . she may be wondering . . ."

Before the 1922 game with Michigan which dedicated the present Vanderbilt stadium, McGugin said to his squad: "You are going against Yankees, some of whose grand-fathers killed your grandfathers in the Civil War." Underdog Vanderbilt fought and clawed to a scoreless tie. The

41

players didn't know, or had forgotten—or didn't care—that McGugin's own father had been an officer in the Union army.

An illustrative McGugin story, to make his players take advantage of opportunities when they occurred, concerned a bumble-bee that was floating around in the clover blossoms when an old bull gobbled him up. " 'I will sting this bull and teach him a lesson,' " Dan would quote the bee as saying. "But then the bee decided it was so cozy and warm inside the bull that he would take a nap and sting the bull when he woke up. And you know, when the bee woke up, the bull was gone."

McGugin used sly methods of stimulating players to super-effort. "In my first varsity year, the night before we played Georgia Tech," said Pete Gracey, 1931 Vanderbilt All-America center, "Coach McGugin casually walked up to me in the lobby of our hotel, put his arm around my shoulder and sorta whispered: 'I was with some Atlanta newspapermen this afternoon and I told them you were the finest sophomore center I had ever coached. I hope I haven't made it embarrassing for you.' We beat Tech, 49 to 7. Afterward I talked to seven other players and you know, Coach McGugin had told them all the same thing he told me."

In his press relations, McGugin was way ahead of his time. Few colleges employed athletic publicity directors then; indeed, many coaches were suspicious of sportswriters from other cities, fearing they were spies. McGugin not only made them welcome, but none left his practice, or his office, or his home, without a story. He was the most quoted coach in the South, a distinction Bobby Dodd of Georgia Tech now enjoys. Other "McGugins of today" in this respect are Lou Little, retired at Columbia; Bud Wilkinson, Oklahoma; Forest Evashevski, Iowa; Red Sanders, UCLA, and Jim Tatum, North Carolina.

42

McGugin with tongue in cheek was a decided contrast to modern coaches, most of whom are as serious as they sound. Dan could fraternize with his players freely and yet command their respect. Purposely he would mispronounce words or affect an unsure manner of speech to a new group of players.

"I want all players to meet at the 'Fire House' for the pep rally," he might say.

"Coach, do you mean the Fire Hall on Broadway?" a boy would ask.

"No, no," McGugin would say. "The Fire House over here—Fire Delta Theta."

Oddly, McGugin would not call a boy by his nickname, fearing he might not like it. To him, it wasn't "Nig," it was "Meredith"; it wasn't "Doc," it was "Oliver."

The reserves, or B team, were McGugin's favorites. At the end of almost every practice he would praise their spirit and hustle and conclude with the remark: "Who knows but what Team B will start Saturday?" Many times the reserves almost got up the nerve to answer in unison, "Team B knows"—but they never did.

When McGugin thought his ball-carriers were hogging the limelight, he might call the varsity eleven together for a vote on the question: Which is more valuable to the team, the line or the backfield? Usually the line would win, seven votes to four.

At the beginning of fall practice, if Dan saw a freshman who was a vicious charger, he would quietly approach one of his top senior linemen and ask him to go over and show "this green, awkward boy" how to charge. When the senior was knocked flat on his tail, McGugin always managed to be busily engaged elsewhere on the field.

No joke at all were McGugin's weak kidneys. He had the habit of drinking lots of water throughout a game, and in his later years few stadium spectators realized that his big canvas-bottom chair on the sidelines had a built-in pottie.

McGugin had few equals for restoring a player's morale. After winning Southern championships in 1921, 1922 and 1923, Vanderbilt was upset early in the 1924 season by Tulane, 21 to 13, a game which Clark Shaughnessy says was the "birth of the Sugar Bowl," explaining: "Until then, New Orleans didn't take football seriously." Tulane's hero was Brother Brown, who repeatedly outran Vanderbilt defenders. Returning to Nashville by train, McGugin called to his drawing room the safety man who had missed some vital tackles.

"Where were you when Brown got away?" McGugin asked.

"I just don't know, Coach," said the boy, very nervous. "I just couldn't get to him."

After a pause, McGugin patted the boy on the shoulder and said solemnly: "That was all right. I yelled at him to stop myself, but he just kept on running."

Then came a big smile. The joke got the game and the disappointment off the boy's mind.

On this same trip Tom Ryan, Vanderbilt's ace fullback and punter, missed the train from New Orleans and was a day late for practice. Coach McGugin said the squad would have to vote on whether Ryan could rejoin them. Of course, the other players knew the team couldn't do without him, but they went down to the end of the field to hold a vote while McGugin privately tried to fire Ryan up.

"What would you do," Coach asked, "if a fellow said maybe you were yellow?"

"I would stomp him," Ryan said.

"Well, suppose I said you were yellow?"

Although a bit startled, Ryan said: "Sir, that would have to go for you, too."

McGugin reflected for a moment, rolled his eyes and spoke mildly: "Tom, you make me think of a certain Indian

44

out West. When he saw his first locomotive, he said he was going to lasso it. I admire your courage, but you've got mighty pore judgment."

Tom had to laugh. The next week he played the best game of his career.

McGugin was a genius for adapting material to his system, the short punt formation. Ryan, for instance, played offensive fullback and defensive end. Often in close games Vanderbilt used only thirteen or fourteen players. The eleven starters played the full sixty minutes in upsetting Minnesota, 16 to 0, in 1924.

Lynn Bomar, an All-American end, actually played blocking back on offense and line-backer on defense. McGugin utilized the big blond (six feet, two inches and weighing 208 pounds) to maximum efficiency at catching passes, running interference for the ball-carrier and, on defense, stopping opponents at the line of scrimmage. As an extra touch, Bomar kicked off, usually between the goal posts. He was the winningest player I ever saw, never to carry the ball. In 1925, Bomar was all-professional end with the New York Giants. Jess Neely, Rice coach and 1922 Vanderbilt captain, said recently: "I've never seen a football team that Bomar couldn't have made."

It's especially satisfying to see two blockers like Bomar and Southern California's Ernie Pinckert recently elected to the National Football Hall of Fame.

Bronko Nagurski as a Minnesota tackle in 1929 is my No. 1 college lineman (I never saw Cal Hubbard at Centenary or Geneva). The Bronk's later exploits as a fullback are well-known, but I have an unforgettable mental photograph of him starting from twelve yards back and catching Jess Thomas, Vanderbilt's fastest 1929 halfback, after he had raced sixty-four yards with an intercepted pass.

My own all-time, all-purpose college backfield performer is Charlie Trippi for University of Georgia in 1942, 1945 and 1946, a bewildering ducker, dodger and maneuverer who wrecked the equilibrium of opposing teams with his incredible escapes. Trippi in his prime removed the ceiling on what one man could mean to a football team. There have been runners as good, and passers and punters even better, but I never saw one player who could do all three things as well. What made this triple-threater the "decathlon champion" of football in my book is that he was also a first-rate blocker, and Coach Wally Butts cannot remember him missing a tackle or allowing a completed pass in his territory during his entire college career.

Trippi told me that on the spring day in 1941 when he arrived in Athens, Georgia, on his first train ride and felt the warm sun and smelled the fragrant air after a lifetime in the mining town of Pittston, Pennsylvania, he promised himself: "I'll never leave here." He still lives there, after an outstanding pro career with the Chicago Cardinals.

Another personal opinion, shared by many former players and coaches in the South, is that a superb natural athlete named Jack Wakefield would have been one of the great players of all time had he remained in college. He left Vanderbilt after a 1923 freshman season, entered professional baseball and shortly thereafter committed suicide in Memphis. Wakefield, six-one and 197 pounds, was thick, powerful, fast, arms like a gorilla, enormous hands, and he could pass fifty yards with either. There was nothing on a football field Jack couldn't do, and do it skillfully and at the same time savagely. He was the most punishing, destructive football competitor I ever saw.

Another extraordinary athlete on the same 1923 Vanderbilt freshman team, rated just a notch below Wakefield, was Andy Reese. He too entered professional baseball, playing for years with the New York Giants. Had they stayed in school, both probably would have been in a 1924 backfield with their brothers, All-American Hek Wakefield and All-

46

Southern Gil Reese. Never, I'm sure, would there have been two sets of brothers with such ability on the same team. This was one of Coach McGugin's saddest disappointments.

Jack Wakefield and Lynn Bomar had prepped at Fitzgerald & Clarke School at Tullahoma, Tennessee, coached by Wallace Wade, and in 1921 Wade joined McGugin as an assistant in a "package deal." In contrast to the easygoing McGugin, Wade was cold and feared by the players, yet this combination developed unbeaten teams two years straight. In 1923 Wade applied for the University of Kentucky head coaching vacancy, became impatient over the long deliberation of the selection committee and walked out after telling them that wherever he did go, he would never lose to Kentucky. He went to University of Alabama, produced three Rose Bowl teams in eight years, then to Duke—and Kentucky never beat him in eight meetings.

Many tales are told about Wade's toughness (his players and assistant coaches called him "The Bear"), but a true one is sworn to by Tommy Prothro, Oregon State head coach who was a quarterback at Duke in 1939-40-41. Wade liked to drive his own automobile ahead of the team bus on short game trips, taking with him the starting backfield. On one of these drives, Wade stopped for the bus to catch up, pulling over near the edge of a ditch. Too near, in fact, and the front wheels were headed ditchward.

"Tell him," Prothro nudged.

"No, you tell him," whispered George McAfee.

Nobody would. When they resumed the trip, the car plopped over. They left it there and hitch-hiked to the game.

After Wade (Lt. Col.) returned from World War II, he mellowed. He was no longer feared. When he asked one of his former players, Billy Hickman, how he liked watching his (Wade's) single wing formation, Hickman said: "I'd rather sit in a dentist's chair."

47

Wade just smiled.

Maybe Dan McGugin could have mellowed Wade earlier if he had subjected him to the gags he pulled on Fielding Yost, long-time University of Michigan coach. But Yost happened to be McGugin's brother-in-law, and couldn't do much about it, because—

When Dan married a Nashville girl, Virginia Fite, in 1905, Yost was his best man, and there he met Virginia's sister, Eunice, who became Mrs. Yost.

Serious, straight-thinking Mr. Yost used to rush to Nashville at the end of Michigan's football season to see Vanderbilt wind up against Sewanee on Thanksgiving Day. Then he and McGugin would go to the American Football Coaches Association convention. One year Yost was to deliver the convention's principal address, and on the long train ride he insisted on rehearsing the speech as McGugin listened—so often that McGugin knew it by heart. As the coaches' meeting opened, a discussion arose on the floor and the chairman asked McGugin to come to the rostrum and make some remarks on the subject. McGugin responded by giving Yost's speech in its entirety. When brother-in-law Yost's time came, he had to improvise as best he could.

On another occasion, McGugin and Yost were with friends on a duck hunt in Arkansas. Yost was an avid historian, and was said to have been the first man in America to declare that Doc Cook, once heralded as the discoverer of the North Pole, was a fraud. Yost was a champion of the true discoverer, Commodore Peary.

At dinner one evening, McGugin framed it that someone should start a discussion about Cook and Peary. After informal debate, it was suggested that a ballot be taken to see how the individuals stood on the matter. They voted, with the result 16 to 3 in favor of Peary as the genuine discoverer.

As expected, Yost leaped to the floor and orated for forty

minutes for the purpose of convincing the negative three. When he finished, McGugin suggested they vote again.

This time Cook won, 18 to 1.

Grantland Rice once wrote: "I have known a long, long parade of football coaches, but I never met one who combined more of the qualities needed to make a great coach than Dan McGugin carried."

As squads became larger and there was less and less personal contact between coach and player, McGugin found it harder to win. Football was changing. Most coaching futures are shaped by how many games the team wins or loses, but not often does one game change the course of events.

McGugin had announced his retirement in September, 1934, to take effect at the end of the season. On the morning of the final game, against Alabama in Birmingham, he called Blinkey Horn, sports editor of the Nashville *Tennessean,* and me to his room and told us we could prepare a story, to be released the following Sunday, that line coach Josh Cody was succeeding him as head coach. But that afternoon Alabama, bound for the Rose Bowl, rolled up a 34-0 score and could have made it 60 to 0. Alumni went to work and brought in Ray Morrison, stellar 1908-11 Vanderbilt quarterback who had gained fame as the ringmaster of Southern Methodist University's "aerial circus."

Morrison's 1937 team missed the Rose Bowl bid by losing its final game to Alabama, 9 to 7, on Sandy Sanford's fourth-quarter field goal. It was the last of the "iron man" teams, with six linemen, including All-America center Carl Hinkle, playing four 60-minute games. But it's remembered best as the last college team to win a game with a hidden ball trick, beating Louisiana State, 7 to 6.

On the day before the game, Morrison told me in confidence that something was going to happen on the third play, if Vanderbilt received the kickoff. But he would say no more. A few minutes before the game Morrison told the referee the type of trick play to be attempted; he wanted to establish its legality. But somehow it happened on the second play, instead of the third, and the worst fooled man in the stadium, perhaps, was the referee. Vanderbilt had the ball at midfield, second down and four yards to go. The signal-caller bent over in the huddle and whispered two words: "Henry Frnka." (Frnka was then Morrison's assistant, later coach at Tulsa and Tulane, and the trick play was his suggestion.)

Vanderbilt lined up in the T. The quarterback, Dutch Reinschmidt, spun and headed on a wide left sweep, preceded by a swarm of blockers. It appeared that he would be thrown for a heavy loss. But—he didn't have the ball. Down on the 25-yard line a Vanderbilt lineman, Greer Ricketson, was loping toward the goal and there wasn't an LSU player within twenty-five yards.

To this day not more than a handful of the 20,000 people on hand that day know how the play worked. Indeed, some of the players who pulled it are not in complete agreement. Ricketson, a tackle who lined up at right guard for this particular trick, explains it this way.

"When Reinschmidt took the ball from center, he quickly placed it on the ground behind our left offensive guard, Bill Hays. I pulled out from right guard as if to join the interference. Just as I got behind Hays, I tripped—accidentally on purpose—over him. He was squatting over the ball by then like a hen hatching an egg. I picked up the ball and simply ran down the right side of the field, thinking above all else not to stub my toe."

Morrison, along with the late Frank Murray of University of Virginia and Marquette, were the most scholarly men I've known among football coaches. Both were the faculty type. I've always thought Morrison, to whom recruiting was distasteful, would have been a tremendous success as purely a play designer and offensive coach in pro football. He liked to spring some bold maneuver, to pull the unexpected, such as lining his team up to make the opening kickoff from one side of the field, then suddenly passing the ball laterally to the other side.

I almost had Morrison talked into something drastic just before the 1939 Vanderbilt-Tennessee game, and still regret that at the last moment he declined, with regrets.

Tennessee had won twenty straight games. Vanderbilt had lost five that season. The gamblers were laying 8 to 1 Tennessee would win and 8 to 5 Vanderbilt wouldn't score. It was an extreme situation calling for extreme measures and I wanted Morrison to come on the field for the pregame workout with a baseball fungo bat in his hand and his players dressed in baseball suits. How would it have affected the Tennessee players? And the coaches?

I still wonder.

And Don't Forget—He's A General

From nothing, I've watched University of Tennessee over the past thirty years become the winningest team in college football. It's all due to one man: Bob Neyland. Rather, General Robert Reese Neyland, for on him the name—and the gold star—fit.

Neyland liked to command, whether it was Stateside in the Army engineers, or at the Port of Calcutta in World War II, or coaching. He wanted the responsibility, for he was a perfectionist and a disciplinarian, and he was going to get the job done, and you were going to work for him—or else. And if you didn't like the way he was doing things, get the hell out of the way.

Lots of boys who liked it, or grew to like it, today are head football coaches. Tennessee has displaced Notre Dame and Neyland has supplanted Rockne as the maker of coaches. Besides innumerable staff assistants all over the map, there are in the big time such Neyland-trained head coaches as Bobby Dodd, Georgia Tech; Murray Warmath, Minnesota; Phil Dickens, Indiana; Bob Woodruff, Florida; Bill Meek, Southern Methodist; DeWitt Weaver, Texas Tech, and Jim Myers, Iowa State.

Plus, of course, the man the General wanted and got as his successor, Bowden Wyatt, the 1956 national Coach of the Year. It's suspected that Neyland saw in Wyatt, 1938 Tennessee captain, his own self twenty-five years younger, when he had played the same position, end, at Army. Wyatt has modeled after Neyland even to the point of dressing like him, and while the civilian may not be as stern in his dealings as the soldier, neither man is much jokester.

In his early coaching days Neyland was difficult for sportswriters, especially his home sportswriters in Knoxville. Football is serious business to lots of coaches, but to Neyland it was war, and propaganda was a weapon to be used in the all-out effort for victory. His No. 1 motto: "Never underestimate an opponent." So he struggled desperately and used any means trying to gain the role of underdog.

Today many people object to the publication of game odds or so-called point spreads in newspapers, feeling that it encourages gambling. Maybe it does. But at the same time it discourages ridiculously pessimistic pregame "pore-mouthing" by coaches and it does give an unbiased view as to the valid favorites for the upcoming Saturday.

Neyland regarded football as closely akin to war because "the game is nothing more than a series of actions, mistakes and miscalculations." He operated on the principle that the team making the fewest mistakes will win.

Defining football play as a "compound of errors," Neyland drilled into a squad his gospel that there are more ways to score on defense than on offense.

"There are only three ways to score on offense, (1) run, (2) pass or (3) kick," he said. "On the other hand there are five ways to score on defense: (1) intercepted pass, (2) safety, (3) recovered fumble in air, (4) blocked kick and (5) punt return."

Neyland emphasized the alert defensive frame of mind as no other coach I've known.

"I simply cannot understand why so many football teams

feel like they just have to score the first time they get their hands on the ball," Neyland says. "Most of them seem to feel that possession of the ball is to be desired above everything else. I disagree.

"Say that you do get the ball early in the game down on your 20-yard line. You throw everything you have in your attack trying to score from there. Well, look how the percentage operates.

"First, you're liable to lose the ball on a fumble. The more you run with the ball, the greater the fumble possibility.

"Then, if you do succeed in moving the ball to midfield and there decide to try some passes in an effort to keep advancing, you may get a pass intercepted.

"Finally, if you *are* fortunate enough to move the ball to the other team's 30- or 25-yard line, even down that far—well, it's quite possible that you may stall and lose the ball on downs there.

"So, isn't it a lot easier to just punt the ball down there in the first place?"

Neyland bases his concept on logic rather than patience.

"If one team is so much superior to another that it can score from 'way out, that it can launch an 80-yard scoring drive the first time it gets the ball, then the odds are that it can score even easier later in the game," he reasons. "Why be in such a hurry, why take chances deep in your own territory at the start of a game?"

A newspaperman's best chance to get Neyland to talk, in his coaching heyday before he retired to the athletic directorship, was at Southeastern Conference meetings, or coaches' conventions, arguing points with colleagues. Intelligent and forceful, I never saw him come out second-best even in parliamentary scrimmages with college presidents. Fact is, the General came—and comes—closer to saying what's what at his university than any football coach I've known.

54

Neyland isn't a showman. In the coaching profession he's one of the marveled-at exceptions in his ability to refuse to make speeches or radio-TV appearances. And even his old Army teammate and warm friend, President Dwight Eisenhower, couldn't get Neyland to play golf. That's about the only game Neyland never could whip.

At West Point, Neyland was not only an outstanding end, but one of the best baseball pitchers in Army history and the Academy's heavyweight boxing champion. A few weeks after graduation he was invited to a house party on Long Island, an affair the handsome young Texan had looked forward to with pleasure. But when the party got around to play time, Bob found out he couldn't do anything.

Nobody wanted to box with him. Nobody wanted to pitch baseball. Nobody wanted to block or tackle.

So Neyland soon thereafter took up golf and tennis. The latter he mastered. But after much, much practice and many lessons, he admitted that golf had defeated him, and he quit, giving me these reasons:

1. There was no man-to-man combat.

2. A person could not make his opponent play the kind of game he wanted him to play.

3. It was too long between shots, and not enough action.

Neyland has a fondness for axioms and gems of wisdom, and makes up a few of his own. Such as: "The first law of living is, 'Don't kid yourself.' "

One time I asked him what proverb or saying had influenced him most. He quoted Kipling's "If you can meet with triumph and disaster, and treat those two impostors just the same . . ."

Among Neyland's favorite persons is Herman Hickman, who played under him at Tennessee and, in one respect, exceeded all proteges who followed The General into the coaching profession by attaining the hallowed chair at Yale. When they get together, invariably there's "you-top-this-one" competition in a literary vein.

Hickman might recite the instructions of former West Point coach John McEwan to an inquiring player who wanted to know what he should do after being handed the ball on a certain new play: "Simply dispatch yourself with the utmost precision and proceed as far as your individual excellence will permit."

And Neyland might parry with a phrase describing an opposing player blocked into a somersault: ". . . a perfect case of fortuitous juxtaposition."

From his very first coaching years at Tennessee, Neyland manufactured maxims or lines of thought which he pounded into his players. And it wasn't until just recently that I heard how one backfired for awhile. The confession was related by Harry (Hobo) Thayer, one of the best tackles Tennessee ever had and team captain his senior year:

"In 1929 we had a bunch of sophomores, and beginning with the very first game of the season, just before we went on the field Major (at that time) Neyland would tell us that our opponent couldn't beat us, because we had the 'superior background.' He never varied that theme. It was the same thing every Saturday.

"Finally we came up to the last game of the season undefeated, and this was the big one, against Vanderbilt. We players were all stretched out in the dressing room, trying to relax, and waiting for 'The Bull' to come and make his talk. That's what most of us called Major Neyland back then. Gene McEver, another sophomore, looked over toward me and said, 'Wonder what The Bull is gonna' tell us today?'

"I said, 'Well, one thing sure, it won't be about 'superior background.'

"Tennessee hadn't beaten Vanderbilt since 1916 and I couldn't figure him even mentioning anything about background. But danged if he didn't show up about ten minutes before kickoff time, start his speech—and go right into that background stuff in nothing flat.

"Well, McEver and Bobby Dodd smother their laughter by turning their heads down on the mattresses, where all of us were stretched out. But I just busted out laughing. I couldn't help it.

"The Major was furious. He glared at me, wanted to know what was funny. I tried to avoid answering but he forced me to, and I had to say just what had happened.

"He didn't say a word. He wrote down the first team on the blackboard. I wasn't listed, though I had started every game up to then. He wrote down the second team. I wasn't listed there, either. We hurried out on the field and I got a blanket and sat on the bench as the first teams ran signals.

"Our captain, Herc Alley, had gone to the center of the field for the toss. When he came back, and our players ran out to line up for the kickoff, The Major turned to me and snapped: 'Get on out there. I guess you were right.'"

When a man is both General and Coach, he encounters few instances of insubordination, but during the week before the Tennessee-Alabama game a few years ago, a mysterious culprit was running Neyland crazy. Each day The General would chalk on the locker room blackboard a diagram and then print under it, "WE'LL BEAT ALABAMA." And each afternoon, when the coaches and squad came back in from practice, written on the blackboard was this addition: "Like——we will."

Naturally Neyland was furious. And his line coach, Murray Warmath, was distressed, feeling sure the offender might be a star tackle. Neyland hid a "detective" in the room and the prankster was caught, a wingback who was promptly dismissed from the squad.

Alabama became the big game on Tennessee's schedule, and vice versa. In the late 1920's it was Neyland against Wallace Wade, a rivalry that continued when Wade moved to Duke. Then it was Neyland vs. Frank Thomas, and through the 1930's and on into the 1940's I thought the

57

Tennessee-Alabama game annually packed as much wallop as any series in college football.

Neyland was the foremost exponent of the single wing formation. Thomas, a quarterback under Rockne, used the Notre Dame box and the single wing, later changing to the T-formation. I considered Thomas without a peer directing a team from the bench. Many otherwise competent head coaches are not at their best tactically during the actual playing of a game, and depend heavily on their assistants, at least two of whom are advising by telephone from the press box. Thomas could meet sudden situations and readjust quickly and effectively.

The T-formation was brand new to Alabama when it met Boston College in the Orange Bowl in 1943, and within the first five minutes Boston College led, 14 to 0. Thomas changed his end play and Alabama recovered its poise, winning 37 to 21.

Thomas was the only coach I've known who had his players remove their jerseys and shoulder-pads between halves of a game and take a sponge bath. He insisted it refreshed them.

For getting the absolute maximum out of his material in one game, Thomas provided the finest coaching feat I've witnessed when his 1944 team played Duke in the Sugar Bowl, losing 29 to 26. The Alabama squad was made up mainly of freshmen, either too young for the military draft, as yet uncalled, or already rejected as physically unfit. Duke, with Navy V-12 personnel, possessed all the known superior assets: size, depth, speed and savvy. Alabama hitched everything to an 18-year-old freshman passer, quarterback Harry Gilmer, a leaping blond rawhider who that afternoon completed eight for eight. Two of his spectacular soaring beauties spun 57 and 42 yards to set up touchdowns, and in the final seconds another completion, for 32 yards, saw the receiver headed for the

Duke goal and pulled down by a last, lone tackler just as the gun sounded. Thomas rated Gilmer the best college passer he ever saw, with the remarkable faculty of being able to take in the whole field with one quick sweep of his eyes, and throwing to the man who was open. Five of his eight completions in the Sugar Bowl were "hits" on secondary targets when his original receivers were covered.

I traveled with Alabama on many bowl trips. One time at the Cotton Bowl in Dallas, Frank's good friend Dick Andrade arranged a party for the visitors at the sumptuous estate of zillionaire Clint Murchison. One 'Bama football player, after touring the huge home, exclaimed: "Have you seen the upstairs? Man, even the bathrooms have bathrooms!"

After Alabama whacked Southern California, 34 to 14, in the 1946 Rose Bowl game, I was sitting with Frank in the dressing room, deserted except for two student managers collecting dirty game gear and the trainer packing his equipment. A policeman entered, carrying a piece of wood, and walked up to Thomas and said, proudly: "Coach, would you like to have a piece of the goal post to take with you?"

"I believe not," Tommy said. "I think I've about gotten in all my kindling."

At that time I didn't get the full meaning of his words. A heart condition and high blood pressure downed him shortly thereafter. Frank Thomas tried to direct the 1946 team's practices from a trailer, but resigned before the season ended, and died in May, 1954.

The Battle Of Atlanta

I've marveled at Robert E. Lee Dodd ever since that September afternoon in 1927 when I saw him for the first time. He was eighteen, lanky, shambling, big-footed, and I'm not sure he could have run the length of a football field in fifteen seconds. The well-built boy with him, Paul Hug, his best pal, looked like Mr. Universe, and Coach Dan McGugin was trying to get these two prospects from Kingsport, Tennessee, enrolled at Vanderbilt. He asked me to take them to a movie and to help keep an eye on them for a day or so. But the ugly duckling of the two boys found he didn't have enough credits; Dodd and Hug wanted to stick together, and they wound up at Tennessee.

Hug, inevitably, became a fine college end. But this Dodd became merely the smartest field general I ever saw in action, All-American quarterback in his senior year, and as I look back it still puzzles me.

Certainly Bobby was an exceptional forward passer and a marvelous punter. But he was a bold gambler on the field and a relaxed nonconformist off the field, and how he thrived under strict, ultra-conservative Bob Neyland is, to me, one of the modern sports miracles. Dodd just had his own way of doing things, and he still does, to the wonderment—and perhaps the envy—of many of his coaching rivals.

"At Tennessee, there was a rule that players got only one glass of milk at training table supper," Bobby told me. "I liked milk and I slipped out every night almost and drank two or three glasses, sometimes a quart. I said to myself back then that if I ever coached, my players would get all they wanted to eat and drink."

Today Georgia Tech players can go through the food line two or three times if they want to. "At first new boys will stuff themselves," Dodd says. "But when they realize there's plenty and they can have all they want, it's surprising how normal their appetites become."

Liberal feeding is one reason for Dodd's marked success as a recruiter. But mainly it's that he tries to take the drudgery out of football. In winning eight straight bowl games the rascal has made a joke out of strict training. All the married players' wives make the trips and the only rule is that all players be in their rooms by midnight. The 1956 team took an 11-day Christmas vacation, reassembled and worked out twice and beat a good Pittsburgh team in the Gator Bowl, 21 to 14. Moreover, the first two Tech teams hadn't scrimmaged since early September.

"The idea is to have as much fun as possible and still play a good game," Bobby says. "That's always what I wanted to do when I was in college."

"Nobody else in the country can coach like Dodd and win," Bear Bryant of Texas A. & M. asserted.

Another coach added: "I want to find the fellow who coaches like Dodd, and play him. Not Dodd—just somebody like him."

But I've never known anybody just like Dodd, as a player or coach. He was unorthodox, he took long chances, but he seldom was made to look bad. He seemed to have the knack of outguessing an opponent, of calling the one single play that fitted the game situation. "It was more genius than brains," Bob Neyland once told me. "I do not believe that Dodd arrived at his decisions by any deductive process, but unerringly played his hunches."

One of these hunches, in the very last game of Dodd's college career, had a lot to do with Bill Alexander picking him as an assistant coach at Georgia Tech. As Tennessee's quarterback Bobby violated a basic Neyland principle by calling a pass against Vanderbilt deep in his own territory, so deep that he found himself behind his own goal line, circling and twisting out of the grasp of frantically clawing figures. Just as Dodd seemed to be smothered, he threw the ball to halfback Buddy Hackman at the 25-yard line and Hackman trotted all the way for a touchdown. The daring, impromptu act was widely publicized and was all Alexander had to know; a few weeks earlier his chief scout, Mack Tharpe, had confessed to arriving late to scout North Carolina in a game against Tennessee, but claimed that in talking to the Tennessee quarterback, this boy Dodd, after the game he had gained much better information than he could have obtained by watching the Tar Heels himself.

The truth is that Dodd loved to gamble, and not just as a football quarterback. After going to Atlanta he developed an insatiable fondness for playing golf and cards— for money. Big money. Among amateurs, there was no cooler cookie at making a clutch putt or going for high stakes in gin rummy. By nature and temperament he was a winner, an expert at gamesmanship. It was not only profitable but it was exhilaratingly pleasant. Then suddenly Bobby quit. Why? He has never discussed it in detail, but he just decided it didn't fit into his way of living. Today he never plays a round of golf or a game of cards. He fishes; he has even fished on the mornings of games. It's his only recreation, and he is often accompanied on the expeditions by his pretty wife, daughter and son. Some friends say Bobby has fished so many lakes and streams that the TVA thought of naming one of its water impoundments for him, but "Dodd Dam" was vetoed.

In the pressureful pursuit of football coaching, Dodd worries less than any man I know. Georgia Tech is a most secure place (three coaches in fifty-three years) and Atlanta a most advantageous football locality. But mainly it's just Dodd's makeup; he has never lost the player's viewpoint and capacity for fun.

Once in the fourth quarter of a game Dodd rigged up and sent in quickly a special play so that Bob Davis, 225-pound senior tackle, could catch a lateral pass and experience the thrill of a touchdown. It's a regular occurrence for the Georgia Tech coaching staff to challenge a group of players to a game of basketball or volleyball, or to a tennis tournament. After every home game, win or lose, the Tech staff and their wives eat at Dodd's home, and no one is allowed to talk football, win or lose.

Dodd's personality is reflected in the Tech team's accent on deception and the element of surprise. "There's nothing boys get a bigger bang out of than making some guy on the other side look silly," he says. "That's why they'll drill for hours and hours on something like hiding the ball. Most people like to act, and faking in football depends largely on the facial expressions of the fakers."

In human relations, Dodd also knows that newspapermen are the happiest when and where they find a good story. Earlier I mentioned that in this respect Dodd is the South's modern McGugin. He's good copy himself, and he shapes such a policy throughout Georgia Tech athletics. I believe Tech was one of the first schools to compile "number of tackles made" in its game statistics, a useful item in comparing linemen. Dodd can even find something news-worthy in the performance and personality of an offensive center, the most "anonymous" player on the field in this era of the T formation. Frank Broyles, Tech assistant who moved to University of Missouri as head coach, patterns after Dodd in his sagacious press relations. If there isn't any news, they'll make some.

I've seen Bobby stop a scrimmage and give a "battlefield promotion" to some B team player who had been wearing out a varsity opponent. He's had more luck with little players, the sawed-off 160 pounders, than any coach I know. Of course there are some who say that Dodd has more luck, period. "If an atom bomb dropped on Atlanta, old Dodd would come up with his pockets full of uranium," was the way one competitor put it. Which doesn't bother Bobby. He believes: "If you think you're lucky, you are."

Dodd's predecessor, the late Bill Alexander, had his share of fun, too. Whenever Alex diagrammed a play, he always chalked tiny "x's" to denote Tech players and huge circles to represent the opposing team.

When the rules committee first ordered all players to be numbered, one of Alex's old boys who was coaching a small college in South Carolina came to him quite disturbed. He contended it would make things too easy for opposing scouts. Alex suggested putting Roman numerals on the jerseys, that there was nothing in the rules against it. Which the fellow did, and almost got fired.

A favorite of Alex was Bill Fincher, a giant Tech tackle who had one glass eye. Often, after two or three plays had been run in a game and some physical contact established, Fincher would surreptitiously slip his glass eye into his hand, then suddenly show his face to the lineman opposite him and growl: "So that's the way you wanna' play, huh?"

Perhaps the severest test of Alex's equanimity came after he married, late in life, and one morning came to breakfast early, ahead of the family. "I'll eat the rest of that barbecue hash I had last night," he told the cook. "Heat it and put it on toast."

The toast appeared with hash on it and Alex ate. Several minutes later he was sipping his second cup of coffee when Mrs. Alexander came in, after first visiting the kitchen, and informed him that he had eaten not hash, but a half-can of dog food.

"Well, it was a little flat, but not bad," Alex said, with insouciant calm.

He had the gift for not worrying about those things about which one can do nothing.

Alex could be gruff at times, and nothing riled him more than criticism of his players. In the locker room after Alabama beat his 1933 team, 12 to 9, on a last-minute pass interception, an assistant coach lacerated the Tech squad for its lapse. Alex couldn't stand it. "Get out!" he thundered at his aide. "This is your team only when it wins. Now it's my team. Get out before I throw you out!"

Georgia crackles the year round with the rivalry between Georgia Tech and Georgia, in nearby Athens. Sportswriters in the metropolis and capital city are caught right in the middle. Through the years Atlanta could, and can, boast some of the best—Ed Danforth, Ralph McGill, O. B. Keeler, Morgan Blake, Edwin Camp, Fuzzy Woodruff, Jimmy Burns, Morris McLemore, Ed Miles, Furman Bisher, Jess Outlar, Bob Christian—and mighty few were not accused at one time or another of being pro-Tech or pro-Georgia. All have taken it in stride, though one of the newer columnists, Harry Mehre, former Georgia coach, could invoke the Fifth Amendment. On the few occasions that Tech has lost a game, wise-cracker Mehre makes himself prominent at Monday morning wakes where he sticks in such gags as: "I still think Bobby Dodd's a good coach."

I can well imagine the Atlanta-like problems which exist for sportswriters in Detroit, where Michigan State has become a power matching University of Michigan; in Los Angeles, as UCLA moved from "inside" to the first sports page, alongside Southern California; in Houston, where ambitious University of Houston challenges Rice Institute's long dominance, and many other cities, including Richmond, Virginia, where sports editors Chauncey Durden and Laurence Leonard try to please the followers of Virginia, Virginia Tech, VMI, William and Mary, Washington and Lee—and U. of Richmond. Too often the reader who charges bias is as unreasonable as a jealous wife. Just as "hell has no fury like a woman scorned," a football writer can treat both sides equally and incur wrath and suspicion from the most fanatical followers on both sides. College football generates the fiercest loyalties in sport.

Georgia's coach, Wally Butts, is the Southeastern Conference's senior head man. He is a little round fellow with a kewpie's build and the countenance of a choir boy. But he showed no mercy in lashing halfback Frankie Sinkwich to stardom and the nickname "Fireball Frankie." He also can be as tender and considerate as a bachelor uncle, and was in the case of Charlie Trippi.

Any time I'm with Butts, I know I'm going to hear a quotable sample of his characteristic homespun humor. Usually it's a tale of woe, deprecating his team's chances. One time between halves of a spring intrasquad game, he told me not to go away, that he was trying something new the second half: "I'm going to line up the linemen back to back, instead of face to face, and see if they block any better that way."

Wally once complained that he needed to get a team manicurist because his players were making "so many finger-nail tackles."

On a preseason tour of Southeastern squads, I was staying overnight in the Butts' home in Athens when a late night telephone call brought the news that Georgia's star end, Harry Babcock, had been injured in an automobile accident. Wally buried his face in his hands and sought forgiveness from his wife, Winnie, for becoming a coach. When I came down to breakfast the next morning Butts had his face in his hands again. "One of our daughters," he murmured, "is going to marry a coach."

A girl reporter once asked Coach Butts if he would explain briefly his team's system. "It's the color system," he said. "We just try to knock down everybody not wearing our color."

One December, Butts got a phone call from a coaching friend who thought his team might be invited to play Georgia Tech in a bowl game. The coach wanted some information on the intricacies of the Tech attack, from the fellow who had faced it more often than anybody else. Wally responded with a very clear, if somewhat simplified picture:

"The center gives the ball to the quarterback, the quarterback gives it to the halfback, and the halfback hauls off for the sideline looking for a place to turn."

Both Butts and Bobby Dodd appear on weekly TV shows in Atlanta during the season. It irks U. of Georgia people that Dodd always refers to the school as "Georgy." And Butts has been known to advise Tech-bound high school athletes to "make yourself famous there, be different, study engineering." That's a jibe at the other, and easier, courses offered at Tech.

Another Southern rivalry within the Atlanta "sphere" is Clemson vs. South Carolina, which for years matched two colorful characters, Frank Howard vs. Rex Enright. Howard still coaches Clemson; Enright has become South Carolina's athletic director.

Enright had lost four straight games in his last season, 1955, when he faced his squad before the Virginia game. "Boys," he said, "we are going to try something new. The minute the game's over, I want you players who're on the field to form this semicircle." (He drew a semicircle on the blackboard.) "I want you players who're on the bench to rush over and close the circle." (He completed the circle with his crayon.) "I'll be in the middle of it and we'll all run like hell for the dressing room."

I don't know how much the gag helped, but South Carolina broke its losing streak.

Howard is a tobacco-chewing wisehead who is not averse to giving away some of the tricks of his trade. "Whenever I'm recruiting a good high school boy," he divulged, "I always tell him he's gonna play in the backfield. When we have him in his first practice, I tell him he's gonna back up our line. After a few days, I sorta sneak up and mention to the boy that if he could play a little offense, he might get to play a lot more. Usually he'll agree to that, and pretty soon I got that sucker playing guard."

Howard himself was a guard.

Names That Fit And Names That Don't

Lots of newspaper people and all photographers talk about one picture often doing the job of a thousand words. Sometimes three or four words can be worth a thousand pictures.

One day I was perusing the paid death notices in the *Banner,* and there in agate type, immediately following the deceased's full name, was his age, fifty-nine, and these words: ". . . better known as 'Good Time Dog.' "

That one phrase alone sufficed for a book of pictures.

With people and animals and things and places, there are names that fit and names that don't. At least, I find it that way, on and off the sports beat.

If I ever write a football drama, the name of the team physician will be Dr. Arch Metatarsal.

I never check into a certain hotel at Columbus, Ohio, without thinking that the name sounds like part of an early-season basketball result: "Baldwin-Wallace 68, Deshler-Wallick 59."

Somehow, the name of the firm that manufactures the Louisville Slugger baseball bat, Hillerich & Bradsby, has the clatter of a bunch of bats en masse, when they are gathered up and rolled over each other.

Did you ever hear of a dog named Clarence? Or Herbert? No. Neither fits.

Foxhunting folks in Tennessee and Kentucky give lots of thought to naming their hounds, figuring the names should suggest muddy roads, gates that have to be unlatched, the smell of wood fires and a white house in an oak grove. In almost any pack there is a "Lige" and a "Doll." One farmer who swapped a mule for three Walker hound puppies pondered for weeks over a choice of names, then went to the Twenty-third Psalm for help. He called them "Surely, Goodness and Mercy." Naturally "Surely" was the male of the trio.

In Atlanta, Ed Danforth knew of a pair of smart Dalmatians who came up with formidable names in keeping with their set. They first were christened Abercrombie and Fitch, but that offered difficulty in calling them in a hurry. Gilbert and Sullivan was the final choice for yard names. In time the coach dogs were referred to as Gilbert Abercrombie and Sullivan Fitch, the latter name proving very satisfactory when stern reproof was desired.

In 1946 the operators of a Louisville hotel planned to name a new cocktail lounge for the winner of the next Kentucky Derby. They envisioned something flavorful, for had the idea been thought of early enough, they could have had the "Old Rosebud Room," the "Bubbling Over Bar" or the "Whirlaway Roof." Damned if the Derby wasn't won by Assault.

I'm positive that Man o' War could never have been the horse he was if his name had been Uncle Miltie. Or Bug Juice.

Race horse owners are confined to sixteen letters and spaces in selecting names. Alfred Gwynne Vanderbilt believes the public appreciates clever choices. His Native

Dancer carried out a Pacific theme; he was by Polynesian out of Geisha. A daughter of Discovery-Buffet Supper was named Self-Service. But Vanderbilt's prize pick was Social Outcast, named for its Thoroughbred parents, Shut Out and Pansy.

Among animals, how fitting the name of the kangaroo! The origin of the word inclines you to suspect Divine Guidance. The fact is that the discoverers of Australia inquired of a native, by pantomime, the name of the pouched mammal with the hind limbs enlarged for hopping and the long thick tail. The native answered: "Kangaroo," an aboriginal expression meaning "I don't know," or "I don't understand what you mean."

And there was the old Negro who remarked: "They musta' had a hard time naming all the animals, cep'n the hawg. Anybody would have knowed it was a hawg."

The Greeks had a word for the fitness of names—"onomatopoeiaist," I think it was. Naturally I don't know how it worked back then, but in our times I cannot imagine the TV intellectual Charles Van Doren achieving such fame if his name had been Gus Flunk.

And Butch Slaughter, one of University of Michigan's many All-American football players, couldn't possibly have been a tailback. He had to be a guard.

For those who contend there's nothing in a name, just suppose the former major league catcher, Matt Batts, had a nephew named Mutt Butts?

I have offered all the foregoing froth as an allegation that three of the best-known football coaches have the worst-fitting nicknames: Red Sanders of UCLA, Bud Wilkinson of Oklahoma and Bear Bryant of Texas A. & M.

Their real names, respectively, are Henry, Charles and Paul.

Sanders' hair, graying rapidly, has never been red. His complexion is dark. He got the name from an uncle who, watching him play grammar school and corner-lot football in Nashville in a red sweater, said: "You look like a scrub red Jersey bull."

But if Red's name doesn't fit, his temperament does. His often cheerless expression cloaks a perception of humor and a pungent facetiousness which seem to trump any bid that tension makes.

When UCLA lured Sanders from Vanderbilt in 1949, he was so little known in Los Angeles that one of the newspapers sourly introduced him to its readers as a "male Caucasian, aged 45." Another newspaper asked if he, a Southerner, were prejudiced or intolerant on the matter of playing Negroes. "I'm prejudiced in favor of any boy who can play football," Sanders answered, "and intolerant of any player who won't block or tackle." When it was suggested that his single wing offense might be old-fashioned, he said: "Maybe it's a horse-and-buggy offense, but I like to think we have a TV set on the dashboard."

Red's own laughter was the loudest at his very first meeting with the UCLA squad. He told the players he was new on the scene, that UCLA was a mighty big place, that he couldn't check on them closely and that he had been told that if a boy were so inclined, he could get into devilment right on the campus. With that a big tackle raised his hand and asked, "Where?"

Conscious of certain sportswriters' allergy to triteness, Sanders with malice aforethought answers their questions with such moth-eaten phrases as "I hope Dame Fortune is with us," "We may not win but they'll know they've been in a fight," "Our escutcheon isn't going to be blemished," etc. Then, after he's had this fun, Red will talk so articulately and which such a sense of what is news that he practically writes the lead paragraph.

Sanders has never kidded himself about the hazards of

72

coaching. When a cheering horde of students serenaded his apartment, pleading for him to stay at UCLA instead of accepting a University of Florida offer, he told them: "No coach in the world is worth all this excitement." But aside to his wife, Ann, he muttered: "Which one has the rope?"

Before he moved West, Sanders said he had always thought Hollywood was a place where a bunch of fellows sat around a swimming pool with a dry martini in one hand and a wet blonde in the other. "But it isn't like that at all," he explains now. "A lot of the fellows in Hollywood don't like martinis."

Red admits he could never feel like a native Californian. "But I feel like an average Californian," he added. "I've been hit three times by a car, have had the virus twice and owe $24,000."

Sometimes I suspect that Sanders long ago pledged to himself that he would meet any so-called crisis in sports competition with some pressure-puncturing saying or deed. I was with him throughout the week before his first Rose Bowl game against Michigan State, January 1, 1954. UCLA's preparation had been particularly arduous because of Michigan State's multiple attack; the UCLA players had to learn more than a dozen types of defense. Which they did, faithfully, but it had been tedious, and they were happy to get it behind them and spend the last two days of practice on offense. Now it was the night before the game, and Sanders had called a squad meeting immediately following dinner at the headquarters in the Town House. "Fellows," Sanders began, "we've just found out that Michigan State has three additional variations of the T which we have not covered. If you have your pencils and tablets—"

Groans were unstifled—until they discovered it was a joke.

Shortly before the kickoff of one crucial game, I heard Red turn to a self-conscious, taut assistant coach who was wearing a new suit and say: "I don't care what anybody says about that suit, you keep on wearing it. It looks all right."

A realist, Sanders has tried to discipline himself not to second-guess his own strategy or mentally replay games. He's not an "if" man. "The best indication of what would have happened is what did happen," he concludes.

Following the unprecedented coaching-from-the-sidelines penalty which changed a 14-14 tie into a 17-14 UCLA loss to Michigan State in the January 1, 1956, Rose Bowl game, Sanders expressed the opinion that coaches never should be running up and down the sidelines. "I don't know about that," objected his old friend Wally Butts. "My alumni at Georgia want me to look real active during a game."

Sanders has as many worries as the next coach, probably more, having been found guilty of recruiting violations in 1956. Yet he was never morose. Visiting a state penitentiary shortly thereafter and called on unexpectedly to say a few words to a group of 1,500 prisoners, many serving sentences of from twenty years to life, Red began: "Men, we've all got our problems. You all are mighty lucky you're not in the Pacific Coast Conference."

I think Sanders' top coaching attribute is his gift for appraising material. He has a knack for determining a player's capabilities, then he expects only the maximum—not the impossible. One of his keenest disappointments was losing Kyle Rote, later an All-American halfback, to Southern Methodist after the San Antonio boy had spent part of a summer term at Vanderbilt. Sanders had Bill Wade, present Los Angeles Rams quarterback, as a freshman at Vanderbilt in 1948 and considered him "potentially the finest single wing tailback of modern times"—before Vanderbilt and Wade changed to the T-formation. But Red calls Ronnie Knox, who played one year for him at UCLA, "the best tailback I've ever seen."

74

As for Ronnie's stepfather, the windy, sometimes pester-some Harvey Knox, who as a Los Angeles *Examiner* by-liner often needled Sanders in print, Red said: "I've never had a harsh word with Harvey. In fact, I hope he goes to heaven. Only thing is, I don't think he'll like God."

Although admiring Sanders' clever repartee, players fear his sarcasm. A UCLA professor once asked him: "Why is it that coaches in other sports are loved by their players, but you're not?"

"I haven't had much time to do any courting lately," Red replied.

I have been around Sanders and Bud Wilkinson enough to know that they're two of the closest friends in coaching. I suspect that Sanders would name Wilkinson as his No. 1 present-day coach, and vice-versa. Both are geniuses for organization.

I predict that Wilkinson's ten-year record at Oklahoma, from 1947 through 1956, with its 40 straight triumphs, its scoring in 116 straight games, its 94 victories against only eight defeats, its ten Big 7 championships in a row, will never be equaled. Unless, perhaps, by Wilkinson himself, who is "not used to being outmaterialed," as he once told a buxom, aggressive young lady snuggling close to him in a crowded elevator at a coaches' convention. Bud does get the best high school players in his state and a few of the best in Texas, but Oklahoma stays on top because of his own excellence.

Wilkinson uses the soft approach. Typical is his routine response to Oklahoma players asking if they could go swimming in the surf in front of their Miami Beach hotel a few days before an Orange Bowl game: "Of course, you can, but it's my opinion swimming tends to have some weakening effect. I don't think I'd do it myself."

They didn't. Wilkinson's mild words were more effective than if he had bellowed a command along with a loud and dire threat of what would happen if it was not followed.

The night before any big game, like Notre Dame, Wilkinson would be found playing what looks, at first, like a game of chess with his quarterbacks. Instead, they're little figurines of football players. Wilkinson takes the "Notre Dame" team and his quarterbacks guide "Oklahoma." Bud sets up the defense and the quarterback makes the call. If he makes what Wilkinson thinks is a poor call, it will be counted as lost yardage; if such a mistake is made once or twice on paper, chances are the boy will remember not to do it in the game.

On the field in practices, Wilkinson employs a point he picked up from Hank Iba, basketball coach at rival Oklahoma A. & M. ". . . Create the situation the player will face in the game, and repeat it until he can react from rote memory."

Like Bobby Dodd at Georgia Tech, Bud stresses the necessity for "acting" to assure surprise. When Oklahoma quarterbacks pitch out to the halfback running wide on the option play, they don't look where they're throwing the ball, even when running at full speed. It's all in the timing.

"Perfection," Wilkinson says, "is not attained at that point at which nothing else can be added, but at that point at which nothing else can be taken away."

What erudite phrasing, and profound wisdom—from a fellow called Bud! The name Galahad would be much more fitting, for practically every football player leaves Oklahoma telling the world that Wilkinson is the finest man he has ever known. "He is an idol to us," said Norman McNabb, "because he represents all the qualities we would like to have."

The adhesive "Bud" appellation was stuck on Wilkinson as a little boy because his father's name was Charles Pat and his was Charles Burnham.

"Bear" is a misnomer for a fellow as handsome and

John (*left*) and I got a little military training in 1917—
at the Wartrace School. Even grammar schools adopted
uniforms in my part of the country when the U. S. went
to war.

WALTER JOHNSON
WASHINGTON AMERICAN LEAGUE

CHARLES E. STREET
WASHINGTON AMERICAN LEAGUE

© 1910 THE SPOR

Gabby Street (*right*), the catcher who held onto Walter Johnson's fast ball, also held onto one thrown from the Washington Monument. It was a thrill for me to see Gabby behind the plate for Nashville in the first professional game I ever saw, in 1916. (*Sporting News photo*)

was all in the family when
elding Yost (*left*) and Dan Mc-
ıgin, brothers-in-law, got together.
ne of those times was before the
'22 Michigan-Vanderbilt game that
dicated Vanderbilt's stadium with
scoreless tie.

Dan McGugin, insisted Grantland
Rice, was surpassed by no man in
his combination of qualities needed
to make a great coach. McGugin
was quite a coach, and quite a guy.

"I've never seen a football team that
Lynn Bomar couldn't have made,"
said Jess Neely recently of his All-
American Vanderbilt teammate.

Bob Neyland, in his early days at Tennessee. No other school had better records over the past thirty years than the Volunteers. Proof, indeed, that the General knew how to marshal his grid forces.

This serious looking chap is Red Sanders. Even as my Vanderbilt classmate in 1927 he was already showing early speed in the humor and gag department.

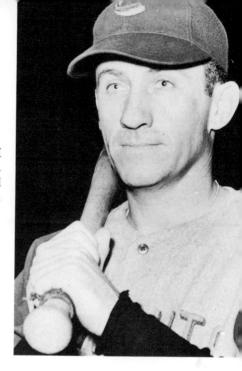

The best all-round minor leaguer I ever saw was Kiki Cuyler (right). As a big leaguer, I always considered him the most underrated of his time.

Clarence Rowland's (*left*) 1930 Nashville team hit 157 homers, had a club batting average of .315, scored 6.6 runs per game. Where did they finish? Dead last!

A gambling man is Bobby Dodd (*right*), the young fellow who had been Tennessee's unorthodox quarterback and today is Georgia Tech's very unorthodox coach.

These ten (*above*) assembled in 1930 to pick the All-Southern team in that year, my first as sports editor. "Linemen" are Bob Phillips, Birmingham; Bill Keefe, New Orleans; Russell; Morgan Blake and Ed Danforth, Atlanta; Harry Martinez, New Orleans; Zipp Newman, Birmingham. "Backs" are Jimmy Burns, Atlanta (later Miami); Fred Digby, New Orleans; Blinkey Horn, Nashville. All are still in sports except those who went to the Press Box in the Sky. Horn died in 1936, Blake in 1950.

It is always a pleasure to be in Herman Hickman's company. Herman, who played under Neyland at Tennessee and became head coach at Yale, told me one of those "mutinous alumni" yarns while he honored me as a radio guest.

Johnny Gooch may never enter baseball's Hall of Fame but he was the best catcher I ever saw at blocking a runner off home plate, and one of the funniest practitioners of baseball's peculiar drollery.

It was fun for me to accompany Red Lucas (*left*) on my first spring training trip in 1931. Red was the Cincinnati Reds' pinch-hitting pitcher and Florida was a fascinating place for a young sportswriter.

Truett Sewell invented the bloo
pitch and once prevented a l
club from going on strike.

Charlie Dressen, as Nashville manager, was "a bantam with unlimited
confidence." Note that club's nickname "Volunteers" gets abbreviated
to "Vols" even on shirtfront.

When MacDonald Smith (*second from left*) was manufacturing golf clubs in Nashville, in the 1930's, he discussed woods with visiting members of the New York Yankees—Sam Byrd, Lou Gehrig, Coach Cy Perkins.

Wallace Wade (*left*) was one of football's fundamentalists. The game was a crusade to Coach Wade, and he taught it with the unyielding force of a field marshal.

Frank Thomas, Alabama's football coach (*center*) in his natural element. He was without a peer at directing a team from the bench.

The most scholarly I've known among football coaches is Ray Morrison.

Nothing riled Bill Alexander more than criticism of his Georgia Tech players, even by an assistant coach.

Carl Hinkle was awarded the silver football for being the Southeastern Conference's most valuable player in 1937. Grantland Rice named no other man from his alma mater on his All-American teams.

All alone, touchdown-bound, was tackle Greer Ricketson as he scored on the famous hidden-ball play that beat Louisiana State in 1937.

The first golf tournament Cary Mid-
dlecoff (*left*) ever won was the
Tennessee Amateur at Belle Meade,
Nashville, 1937. (*AP photo*)

Wally Butts (*above*)—with the countenance of a choir boy—is the Southeastern Conference's senior head man.

No man liked the South as did Larry
Gilbert (*left*). He was making all the
money he needed, so turned down
six chances to manage in the majors.

"Never be meek or morose. Go out there like a bitin' sow."
That's Paul Richards' everyday baseball philosophy.

Adolph Rupp is chiefly responsible for basketball's advancement to its present stature in the South. His Kentucky
clubs are among the nation's powerhouses each court
season.

Ed Diddle's Western Kentucky basketball teams won 663 contests in 35 years—and he is sports' foremost Mr. Malaprop.

friendly and ungrizzly as Paul Bryant. The movies were after him when he went to the Rose Bowl as what he calls "the wrong end" on Alabama's unbeaten 1934 team; Don Hutson, peerless pass catcher, was the right end. Again in 1937, returning to the environs of Hollywood as assistant coach on another Alabama Rose Bowl team, Bryant declined a movie tryout. In 1940, I recommended him to Red Sanders for Vanderbilt line coach. Since then, he has coached at Maryland, Kentucky and Texas A. & M., and everywhere, it's still "Bear."

Bryant got the name when he was in high school at Fordyce, Arkansas, and a traveling show came to town, offering $3 a minute to anybody who would wrestle a trained bear. Bryant's friends goaded him into trying it. His acclaim was encompassed in a sign which hung around the neck of the bear as it walked down the main street of Fordyce. The sign read: I WILL WRESTLE PAUL BRYANT AT THE NEW LYRIC TONIGHT. In the course of the match the bear's muzzle came off. Bryant was flat on his back and the bear leaned over and placed his snout against Paul's turned cheek as the keeper tried to pull him back. Bryant was so scared he ran out of the ring without trying to collect his money.

Sportswriters feast on life stories such as Bryant's. He was the eighth of twelve children in a family that grubbed out a living from unyielding Ozark soil. "It was so far back in the country," Bryant said, "that when you moved, all you had to do was throw water on the fire and call the dogs."

Bryant claims that he and one of his brothers had to catch rabbits for the family to eat, but that the brother had the easier job "because I not only had to catch 'em but run alongside and feel if they were fat."

Even without the exaggerations, Bryant had a rugged boyhood. It's still hard for him to understand how a minor injury can keep a boy out of a football game. In 1935 he played against University of Tennessee with a broken leg—and starred.

Asked as to the physical condition of one of his squads, shortly after he became a head coach, he said: "We're in pretty good shape—except one of our boys has chapped lips."

Bryant is a combination of comedy and candor. One night in New York his old friend from University of Alabama days, Mel Allen, had Paul on his TV program, sponsored by a cigar company. After a few questions and answers there was a pause in the interview as Mel reached in his pocket, thrust a cigar at his guest and said: "Have a smoke. We'll light up now."

Paul recoiled and pushed the cigar back at Allen, stammering: "That thing would make me as sick as a dog."

Acting as if it were a joke, in his frantic effort to recover, Mel made a second effort to hand him the cigar.

"I'm telling you the truth," Bryant reiterated, "that thing would make me as sick as a dog."

Thus ended the interview.

Bryant is a clever as he is frank. When coaching at Kentucky, he visited Army posts in Europe with Fritz Crisler of Michigan, Biggie Munn of Michigan State and Herman Hickman. Knowing full well that many of the troops were familiar with past Kentucky-Tennessee scores, particularly Tennessee's latest victories, Bryant would start off his talk by asking, "Are there any good folks from the old Bluegrass State here?"

Lots of hands would go up, with mingled cheering.

Then Bryant would ask, "Are there any of those Tennessee bastards here?"

That would bring down the house.

I think Bryant injects more of his own fire and sis-boom-bah into a squad than any coach I know. He's electric. When the A. & M. team took the field against Texas Christians, the defending Southwest Conference champion, in 1956, veteran trainer Smoky Harper sidled up to one of the seniors and muttered: "If you all get down near the goal line, put in Coach Bryant. He's really ready."

Almost any coach could put to good use a rhetorical stopper Bryant employs when a hotshot high school prospect doesn't pan out so well in college and interested alumni, or parents, ask why the boy isn't playing.

"You know," Bryant will say, courteously and confidential-like, "I just can't coach that boy."

Is It Charging Or Blocking?

When weighing the sports against each other, you'd better allow for basketball's getting bigger and bigger and bigger.

The game in its youth helped fill, but not nearly to overflowing, what used to be an athletic void in midwinter. It has now spilled over on football's end and baseball's beginning. Before basketball got so big, sportswriters used to get a breath-catching lull between the football and baseball seasons. Columnists hibernated, occasionally shaking a warm coal from the Hot Stove League. Now it is almost necessary to explain the original aptness of that phrase—how it suggested the wintertime gathering place at the railroad station or the general store, and 'tween seasons talk about the "national pastime." The fire in the Hot Stove burns lower and lower. The blaze gets by far its best fanning from dynamic, indefatigable J. G. Taylor Spink, wielding the latest issue of his year-round weekly, *The Sporting News*. But on a daily newspaper, the sports page cannot address very much of itself to the diminishing circle still sitting around potbellied heaters, because so many of

80

the men who once sat there have taken to basketball—and have taken their wives and children to the game with 'em.

In many a family, it is the wife and children who have taken the old man to the game, and have explained to *him* the difference between charging and blocking. And that suggests what seems to me to be the unique feature of basketball's appeal, and a sure sign that the game will grow a lot more yet. Basketball will loom larger and larger on the skyline of sport because basketball is being built on the biggest foundation that exists in sport—school age children, both girls and boys, in virtually every school in the United States.

It occupies this position in the schools and among small-fry because it fills the bill so well. The court itself takes little room, compared with the space requirements of other games, and a single goal can suffice for the recess yard or the home. The inside court is a weatherproof exercise spot that lends itself every day, on schedule, to the school board's commendable purpose of draining off some animal energy in order that a little booklearning may be managed in peace and quiet at other times. Another important point for school people is that injuries are very infrequent in basketball. It's important that girls can get into the act. As for economy, even a very small high school can produce a team that calls for only five players and the same number of substitutes, and the uniforms are no more complicated than underwear and not a whole lot costlier.

At tournament time, whole towns get to meet each other —a circumstance which explains the existence in Indiana of high school gymnasiums that seat more spectators than the population figures for their towns. A state high school basketball tournament is, for many a youngster in my part of the country, the first big adventure and the first real eye-opening trip. One such little-town boy whose team got to the 1957 Tennessee tournament took his first amazed look at the size of the Vanderbilt Memorial Gymnasium, where the tournament was held, and said:

"Wish I had it full of corn!"

Winter, come to think of it, confers a natural advantage on basketball as a spectator sport. The do-it-yourself trend is very strong in America, and a pretty day calls millions to the lakes and the links and the lawnmowers. Football and baseball can be hurt by this competition for the customer's time; basketball hardly at all.

The game has many natural attributes as a spectator sport. Like baseball, it is nifty—but without all the waiting. Like football, it has both teams fully on the field and surging back and forth—but its surges are measured in fast seconds rather than slow minutes. Contests are always played to a decision; last-minute victories are not uncommon; the action is right in the laps of the spectators, sometimes literally. (And the spectators are warm, dry, and back home at a very decent hour.)

The action, most of the time, is sudden and uncharted. Teams have set plays, of course, but more often the scoring is a result of individual reaction, of one or two players' quick sensing of a situation. I've found that fans in all sports prefer individual initiative to the less exciting scene of athletes striving laboriously to carry out to the letter the coach's or manager's standardized patterns.

Another asset, crowd-wise, is that the average basketball team will win its home games a great majority of the time, much more than in any other sport. "It's like Western movies and wrestling," one fan pointed out. "We get to see our heroes prevail." (Odds-makers figure that the home court and the friendly sounds of the home crowd together mean at least six points to a team.)

"On the other hand," said the same fellow, putting his

finger on still another happy comparison, "when we do lose it's not like losing in football. We don't *die*."

This last observation may be close to the reason for basketball's being a strangely infertile field for sportswriters. Basketball remains a *game*—mighty entertaining but never approaching a matter of life or death, nor a way of life, nor a glorious spectacle.

Besides, the sportswriter assigned to this beat must guard against a monotonous sameness in his stories. Basketball goals offer much less possibility for variety of description than touchdown runs and passes do, and the reporter is called upon to describe or at least account for ten or twenty times as many scoring thrusts as there are in football. No matter how impressed the sportswriter is with a guard's defensive play, he's going to have difficulty providing the reader a vivid word-picture. And even the ablest sports department copy editor struggles daily from early December to middle March in his search for a fresh synonym for "basketball" that will fit into a one-column head. He's as weary of "cagers" and "hoop" and "net" as you are.

William F. Fox, Jr., of the Indianapolis *News* is one of the few columnists to create consistently bouncy basketball prose. Often he "di-versifies"; his poetry in season adorns many a high school bulletin board. But Fox would agree that college and professional basketball players and coaches are less colorful subjects than the men and boys in football and baseball. Maybe it's just that the game hasn't matured. Or that its pace is too breathtaking to permit much eccentricity. Or that there have been too frequent rule changes. At any rate it produces comparatively little conversational fodder above the local level—except argument over the rules.

Among basketball's personalities there are a few striking exceptions: Dr. Forrest E. (Phog) Allen, for example, so lively and controversial a figure that retirement can't foul him out of the news. He's still badgering Olympic Games "badgers"; and the migration of Wilt (The Stilt) Chamberlain from his home in Pennsylvania to the University of Kansas must be credited principally to Phog's prescience and persuasiveness. Over a stretch of forty-nine years as Kansas coach (1908-1956) rarely did Dr. Allen visit a city that he wasn't sought for a newspaper interview.

Yes, Phog did make his players take off their socks and shoes and warm their bare feet in front of a roaring fire one hour before game time. ("Keep the feet warm and you keep the nerves of a player calm. I never saw a man with cold feet who wasn't nervous and jumpy.")

Yes, Phog tried to fit every player he had coached into an "ape-man" stance. ("Look at any animal. Whether attacking or defending, he assumes a semi-crouching position. How can you react quickly otherwise? The knees are the only springs in the body. We tell our boys who are learning individual defense to imagine that their arms are cut off at their elbows. When they do this they realize their feet are their best weapon. They'll shift to meet any situation. Look at the weasel-like mongoose: he kills the deadly cobra by grasping its throat after consistently eluding its strike.")

A former Allen pupil, Adolph Rupp, once invited his old coach to address the University of Kentucky basketball banquet. When it was over and he had put Phog on the train, Adolph turned to some friends and said: "Now you see where I got all my baloney."

Rupp is a meaty personality. He also has the highest winning percentage of any coach in basketball: 560 victories, 96 defeats for .854. Unquestionably he is chiefly responsible for the college game's advancement to its present stature in the South. Adolph can evaluate material; it's not true that he eliminates any boy who doesn't have to stoop when entering his office door, although he's reported to have been seen at Lexington's Keeneland race track pari-mutel window one day trying to bet on "the tallest horse."

"The tall man has always dominated basketball and he will continue to do so," Rupp says. "In this respect, basketball is different from any other sport. An All-American back or tackle can't transform a mediocre football team. In baseball, put Mickey Mantle with Kansas City and I don't think you'd see too much difference. But put Wilt Chamberlain with four guys named Joe and you've got yourself a tremendous basketball team."

Yet Rupp wouldn't legislate against the "goons." He thinks raising the baskets from ten to twelve feet would hurt the small player far more than the tall one. Of course there is the brilliantly simple suggestion made by Red Smith (New York *Herald Tribune*) on how to handicap the seven-footers. "Place the baskets just three feet above floor level; that would fix 'em." My own belief is that there should be at least one game for tall—and often awkward—boys to play. They're discriminated against in other sports. What chance do they have as race horse jockeys?

Besides, the height of the baskets may affect the destiny of America. So argued a friend of mine, whose ideas might strike me as preposterous if he hadn't impressed me with his scientific-sounding verbiage. I think what he said was:

"Abnormally tall young men are in a very influential position, genetically speaking, due to their current popularity which is due, in turn, to their pre-eminence in basketball. This contrasts to their frequent former classification—unfortunate and almost always erroneous—as freaks. This ugly label had the effect of reducing their chances for successful courtship, with the result that their effect on the race was minimized. Now the situation is reversed. The boy seven feet tall is everywhere much sought after, and proffered higher education and the more remunerative jobs, and consequently is a hero in the eyes of nubile females, as he perhaps deserved to be all along. Mind you, an appreciable increase in the average height of Americans will eventually reflect all this, statistically."

But back to Rupp. One time Kentucky was playing a small college in Arkansas and led 80 to 3 at the half. Between halves Rupp was talking to the squad and asked, "Whose man is their No. 12 that's scored all their points?"

"He's mine, Coach," answered guard Ralph Beard.

"Well, get on him!" Rupp shouted. "That rascal's going wild!"

Rupp is called "The Baron," and he can be as arrogant as one. Stuck with a technical foul during an important game, he was asked afterward what he thought of the official's action. "Hell, my coaching is worth a technical foul any time," he rasped.

During an Indiana high school tournament, a Big Ten coach was quoted in the newspapers that he was tired of "these carpetbaggers" from the South recruiting Indiana boys. Later, Rupp accepted a speaking engagement in this same town and the newspaper wrote to ask what his subject would be. Adolph replied: "My text shall be, 'A Carpetbagger in the Holy Land.'"

In the matter of basketball's physical contact, he was telling a new freshman group one day that it was "better to give than to receive."

"But, Coach," said one of the players, "I thought the saying was, 'Love thy enemies.'"

"That's the old version," Rupp snapped. "The rules committee changed that."

A lot of wind was taken out of Rupp's sails by the disclosure that some of his players had been guilty of conniving with gamblers and shaving points. Adolph had boasted, you may remember, that the fixers "couldn't touch my boys with a ten-foot pole." How did Rupp survive the scandals? I have reason to believe that Dr. Herman L. Donovan, then president of the University of Kentucky, felt that he himself was responsible, as head of the university, for what went on there, and he should he answerable. In other words, it would not have been upright at all to fire Rupp while remaining in his own job. And maybe it was President Donovan who influenced Adolph to make that trip to New York to appear before Judge Saul Streit, and the grand jury, with such embarrassing results.

The National Collegiate Athletic Association canceled Kentucky's whole basketball schedule for the next year. The Baron and the boys that were left had their $4,000,000 Coliseum to themselves. And they practiced and practiced.

Kentucky has had some awfully good basketball teams since then, and some of the teams were strong tributes to superb coaching rather than to super material. But the degree of domination is less, both as to basketball at Kentucky and as to Kentucky in the region. Their old-time dominance couldn't last forever, even without a scandal. Things were out of balance in Lexington; football deserved a better break and got it under Bear Bryant despite intramural jealousies, and is getting a good break under Blanton Collier. Besides, basketball was sweeping southward like a flood. The hotbeds of basketball were growing too much talent to keep at home.

Bob Polk, in ten years at Vanderbilt, has relied a lot on players from southern Indiana (which happens to be his old home), and from Kentucky and the schools in and around St. Louis. All three of these places are near enough to Nashville for Vanderbilt to get a good many students from them anyway. The basketball players fitted right in, and before long knocked off Kentucky in the Southeastern Conference tournament, an upset of course. More recently, the Commodores' rankings in the nation's "Top Ten" have been earned the harder way of playing heads-up all season.

Meanwhile, other schools in the Southeastern Conference

were stepping up their basketball budgets, beating each other with zest and, on occasion, beating Kentucky with great glee. (There are still some schools which haven't yet followed suit. "Beating Georgia," Rupp said after a Kentucky victory, "is like kissing your sister.") Lexington is still the basketball capital of the whole Southern region between the Appalachians and the Mississippi.

But The Baron's way of besting and often berating the opposition—including officials who seem to him to be taking the side of the opposition—is subdued somewhat. The Wildcats suffer defeat a little more often, and their supporters look on this with less incredulity and amazement than they once would have.

At Bowling Green, Kentucky, only 150 miles from Lexington, is a character more eccentric than Rupp, Ed Diddle of smaller Western Kentucky State College. He's the winningest still-active coach in basketball, 663 victories in 35 years. Diddle's teams and Rupp's teams never play; it would be an all-to-lose, little-to-gain proposition for The Baron. But Diddle is notable in his own right with his towel-tossing habit after each exciting play and his tongue-twisting sayings.

Ed's tangling of words is no act. He just can't help it, and doesn't realize the flaw when he tells an unruly player: "You're just too inde-damn-pendent." Or in passing out new varsity jerseys: "You boys line up, alphabetically according to your height." Or in indoctrinating freshmen candidates: "You all pair off in threes." Or in squelching any rumors of retirement: "I'm going to die with my feet on." But he's no clown; he manages these malaprops while maintaining his dignity.

Diddle in his college days at Centre was a football blocking back, leading interference for the unforgettable Bo McMillin. He brought to Western Kentucky the Centre custom of praying before a game, and Ed always cautioned the boy leading the prayer not to ask for victory, just to ask to play well. Eavesdropping on the pregame huddle one night, he overheard his prayer leader beseech victory. Ed interrupted the supplication, with "— — it, I told you not to do that!"

A basketball pioneer in the South, Diddle's stock in trade is attack—simplified. "There are just three ways to do it," he says. "Down one side of the floor, down the middle and down the other side. I want my boys to fire away; it takes three points to beat two."

As flamboyant figures, both Rupp and Diddle have a younger rival in Lon Varnell, the enterprising University of the South coach at Sewanee, Tennessee. Besides coaching, Varnell operates an automobile dealership, restaurant, hardware store and farm, and often serves as a substitute preacher. Whatever you need, Lon can get it for you whole-sale. He got the 1951 Sewanee team a three-months trip to Europe, all expenses paid, as the guest of the Basketball Federation of Europe. Never one to be underestimated, Varnell, is the only man I know who through wide personal contacts and persistent correspondence has been able to arrive at the selection of an all-time basketball team, college and professional experience combined, which finds little argument among any of the game's closest observers. It's a ten-man squad:

Nat Holman and Bobby McDermott, Original Celtics; Jim Pollard, Stanford and Minneapolis Lakers; Hank Luisetti, Stanford; George Mikan, DePaul and Minneapolis Lakers; Bob Cousy, Holy Cross and Boston Celtics; Bob Davies, Seton Hall and Rochester Royals; Chuck Hyatt, U. of Pittsburgh; Bob Pettit, LSU and St. Louis Hawks; and Tom Gola, LaSalle and Philadelphia Warriors.

The imaginative Varnell has no doubt of his ability to some day talk basketball's rules makers into one final re-volutionary change. "When an offensive player rebounds," he proposes, "require that he must pass the ball off one time before he or his teammates can take a shot at the basket. This would eliminate most of the rough stuff under the goal and tend to lessen the advantage of the tall man."

My own notion of what might develop next in basketball, though not of the magnitude of the revolution wrought by Hank Luisetti's one-hand jump shot, awaits somebody's successful standardizing of the free throw. It is done every whichaway, although the basketball free throw is sport's outstanding example of the set situation wherein nothing is ever the least bit different. The upper edge of the basket is 10 feet above the floor; its back rim is above a point exactly 14 feet 6 inches from the toe of the shooter; the basket's diameter will accommodate the ball with almost 4½ inches of leeway all around.

In football, the technique for placekicking points after touchdown is much more standardized although the situation contains more variables than the free throw. In golf, putting is much more standardized although the distance from clubhead to cup is infinitely varied. In rifle shooting, as taught by no less an authority than the Marine Corps, the best way to hit the bull's-eye was figured out long ago, and the recruit must learn that way.

But coaches in placekicking, in putting, and in rifle shooting are customarily confronted by pupils who haven't done enough of it to be either very good or very fixed in their habits. In basketball, kids get a very early start. And since I've already claimed that's the most important thing about basketball, I guess I ought to let 'em throw the ball at the basket any ol' way they please.

To Be Alive In March—

For me, baseball spring training is the most productive assignment in sports and the most enjoyable stretch of the year. I liked the idea so much that I paid my own way the first time, in 1931, accompanying pitcher Red Lucas, who lived in Nashville, to the Cincinnati Reds' camp at Tampa.

Weather must be a part of the great creative plan for the universe, for to be alive in March is to be born again.

I'm a sun worshiper. It's energizing. Add the aroma of orange blossoms and you have ideally invigorating working conditions, the "write" situation.

Overshadowing even the weather is the multitude of subjects to write about in Florida in the spring. A columnist or baseball writer can gather a full daily supply and also store material he can draw on almost the entire year. He doesn't have to represent a newspaper in New York, Boston, Philadelphia, Washington, Baltimore, Pittsburgh, Cincinnati, Chicago, Milwaukee, Cleveland, Detroit, St. Louis or Kansas City. Some of the most avid readers of major league baseball news live in minor league areas, and are good customers of their minor league club.

Ball players are more accessible during spring training.

They have more time to talk. When in the mood, Ted Williams of the Red Sox might discuss his theory of hitting.

So far as I can tell, there are only two things Williams really likes to do—hit and fish. And I doubt if there has ever been a greater student of the science of hitting and the science of fishing.

"Hitting is all in your eyes and timing," Williams said one day at Sarasota. "The power comes from your forearm, not from your back or your shoulders. Legs have very little to do with hitting. What does it is the snap of the wrist.

"The eye is just as important. You know how your eyes adjust themselves when they move from an object some distance away to anything close by. It's that speed of adjustment that counts most in hitting. I can pick up the ball as soon as it leaves the pitcher's hand and I can follow it up to a point maybe two or three feet in front of the plate. As far as being able to see the ball hit the bat, that's baloney.

"By the time you lose sight of the ball, you know whether it's gonna curve or not. You know just where it's going, and from that point on it's a matter of instinct and timing."

Just as interesting about Williams was his philosophy of competition and life in general, which I picked up once from John Mihalic, an infielder who roomed with him on the Minneapolis club in 1938. It went something like this:

"You're only gonna be as good as you think you are. There was a time when I didn't think I was good enough. That was a big mistake. So I started thinking I was the greatest hitter baseball has ever known. Why? Because I have to think that way to be the greatest hitter. Suppose I'm wrong? Then what? I'll still keep on hitting pretty good and I'll still keep on thinking I'm the best. They can't arrest you for that, can they?"

In Florida a sportswriter may be witnessing the birth of a future star, unconsciously. But he never forgets it. Like the spring of 1940, spent at Sanford, and the 19-year-old left-hander pitching for the rival Florida State League club, Daytona Beach. Name was Stan Musial. Later that year his arm went dead and he was thinking of quitting baseball, but the manager, Dickie Kerr, talked him into trying the outfield.

In spring training I can see bald Enos Slaughter, in his fourties, digging for first base as if he were trying to beat out a vital hit in the World Series, and I recall Slaughter saying, many years earlier: "If I get an extra-base hit that's close, a double or a triple where I have to slide to make it, I owe that extra base to the first eight or ten strides I make breaking from the plate. I don't get it going from first to second or from second to third. Those first few steps are the difference."

And there was the high school boy at Lake Worth, Florida, name of Herb Score, who was striking out fifteen or eighteen batsmen almost every game in the spring of 1952. Lots of scouts were after him, but the scout you remember best is the one who talked not only of the boy's speed, but of his liking for inspirational verse, which he regarded as a tipoff on the youngster's desire and firmness of character, difficult intangibles for a scout to evaluate. Even as an American League ace with Cleveland, Score carries a clipping of the poem, *The Man In The Glass,* by his fellow Floridian, the late Dale Wimbrow, founder of the Indian River *News.*

> *"When you get what you want in your struggle for self*
> *And the world makes you king for a day,*
> *Just go to the mirror and look at yourself*
> *And see what that man has to say.*

> *"For it isn't your father or mother or wife*
> *Whose judgment upon you must pass,*
> *The fellow whose verdict counts most in your life*
> *Is the one staring back from the glass.*

93

"You may be like Jack Horner and chisel a plum
And think you're a wonderful guy,
But the man in the glass says you're only a bum
If you can't look him straight in the eye.

"He's the fellow to please——never mind all the rest,
For he's with you clear to the end,
And you've passed your most dangerous, difficult test
If the man in the glass is your friend.

"You may fool the whole world down the pathway of years
And get pats on the back as you pass,
But your final reward will be heartache and tears
If you've cheated the man in the glass."

A sportswriter staying at St. Petersburg or Tampa can see a game there every day of the exhibition season. Even if he's watching the worst shortstop in the major leagues, if that player is a regular at the position, he is, as general manager Gabe Paul of the Cincinnati Redlegs points out, "the sixteenth best in the world." There are only sixteen such jobs.

It isn't during the games, however, that a sports columnist gets some of his most usable material. If he comes out early enough in the morning, he may find Casey Stengel at Miller Huggins Field, or later at Al Lang Field, sitting on the bench, and approachable. The more writers around, the better Stengel likes it, for he doesn't have to repeat "for stations just tuning in." And the more varied the questions put to him, for the columnist is looking for off-beat stuff rather than spot developments covered thoroughly by the baseball reporters.

One morning as a conversation starter there was a memory-jogger for Casey, about the time he coached the University of Mississippi baseball team, in 1915. They still remember him at Oxford, when he came there to help out his old Kansas City high school coach, Bill Driver, and wearing a long black overcoat and spats.

"When I left, they gave me a goldheaded walking cane," Casey said. "That spring at Ole Miss was a fine thing for me. The experience learned me how to teach young men, and maybe I got something of a jump, because the college men then were like all the young fellows we get now in our Yankee preliminary schools each February. Handling younger fellows involves not only how to teach, but what to teach them.

"Do you know what appeals most to boys? Being shown how to not be a sucker, to not be slicked by the older guys. I show them twenty-four ways not to be suckered."

Stengel refused to disclose even one of the ways. But when he played in the minors there was a foxy old catcher who kept a big chew of tobacco in his mouth and when a rookie at bat got two strikes on him, he would squirt tobacco juice on his shoe. And as the young man turned around to say, "Cut it out!" the pitcher would have pitched and the umpire would be saying, "Strike Three!"

My own belief is that Stengel's foremost managerial quality in guiding the Yankees to so many world championships is the way he delegates authority. Coaching makes the Yankees. Unpretentious Jim Turner's handling of the pitchers is masterful. Without Bill Dickey, I think the odd Yogi Berra might have been a run-of-mill catcher instead of the Most Valuable Player in the American League, 1951-54-55. And quiet Frankie Crosetti, third base coach who's in bed by nine o'clock every night, directs base running and infield play.

The beautiful truth about the Yankees' field supervision is that Turner, Dickey and Crosetti are strictly coaches, extremely well-paid, and neither has the slightest ambition to manage. And Stengel is generous and open in never trying to conceal how much he relies on his coaches.

How do the Yankees maintain a constant flow of exceptional talent? You find the answer at spring training. Those who stick must have more than mechanical ability. They must have the stuff in their mind, and their heart, to absorb the Yankee tradition.

It's quite true that young players with impressive physical assets are discarded because they are judged—mainly by the coaches—as lacking in the qualities to become true Yankees.

By the same token, from what I've seen no Yankee ever is too big to improve—or be improved.

Mickey Mantle was a star in his own right in the spring of 1956. If not the No. 1 name in baseball, he was 1-2-3. But I was eating dinner with Jim Turner on this balmy March night, and Jim's eyes were sparkling, and the reason, he admitted, was Mantle.

"Mickey's beginning to study the pitchers," Jim said. "He's discovering things, little giveaways, little tipoffs. More than that, he's getting a bang out of it.

"He was sitting by me today in the game against the Cardinals. He saw something the pitcher did: the way he gripped his curve. He got it all by himself. Was excited, too, just like a kid. He can see lots of things I can't; has great eyes. It takes a long time to nail something for sure. Lots of players don't have the patience to study closely, to stay with it. But if Mickey keeps this up, if he makes mental notes of the habits and mannerisms of pictures, I tell him he can hit 20 to 30 points higher. But don't go writing stuff like that yet. Let's just see what happens."

What happened was that Mantle led the American League in home runs (52), runs batted in (130) and hitting (.353) —the eighth man in major league history to lead all three departments. And up to 1956, his lifetime major league batting average was .298.

It's in Florida that a sportswriter can observe a new

manager tackling the biggest job of his life, and the little twists he gives it, like Birdie Tebbetts fining any Cincinnati pitcher $25 whenever a hit went through the box which should have been fielded, and putting the money in a fund for a season-end pitcher's party. And in September it's discovered that $400 is in the "kitty," but that Tebbetts has spent $806 for silver bowls he's giving each pitcher at the party, and making up the difference out of his own pocket.

"It's my way," Tebbetts said, "of impressing on these guys that I'm willing to pay my own money to get them to do what I want."

Tebbetts is highly conscious of press relations. "I tell my players," he said, "that if a writer comes up to them, they have my permission to stop whatever they're doing and answer any questions. But I gave them one warning. Never answer a question that ends with, 'Don't you think so?' "

Spring training can be a fruitful period for a writer, looking forward or looking backward. At West Palm Beach, there was Connie Mack, at eighty-nine, in baseball almost seventy years, picking the top thrill of his career.

The wrinkled old gentleman in the high stiff collar flashed back to 1929 and Howard Ehmke, a pitcher on his champion Athletics. Ehmke wasn't the second or even the third best pitcher on the club. George Earnshaw had won 24. Lefty Grove and Rube Walberg each had 18 victories. Ehmke had only a 7-2 record, but he started the World Series against the Chicago Cubs. He not only won, 3 to 1, but he set a new World Series record of 13 strikeouts.

But why did Mr. Mack pick Ehmke?

"I knew that the Cubs feared Earnshaw, Grove and Walberg. I knew that if they beat one of my three aces in the first game, they would get mighty confident, and that impetus might carry them through. The Cubs had some splendid hitters—Hornsby, Hack Wilson, Cuyler, Stephenson, Hartnett, Grimm. I decided that a surprise right at the outset might break their spirit. Too, it turned out to be a cool day for the first game and Howard was a good cool weather pitcher. When Ehmke beat them, it shocked them, and we won, four games to one."

Baseball laughs bloom in the spring, too. There's no grieving over losing; every team's in first place until the season opens. But to oldtimers other things might seem to change.

"You see so few ball players around the hotel lobby at night," ex-pitcher Waite Hoyt, the broadcaster, said to Cincinnati coach Jimmy Dykes. "What are they doing?"

"The same thing we were doing thirty years ago," Jimmy said.

As for curfew, and violation thereof, when Dykes managed the Chicago White Sox he devised a highly effective system of dealing with night owls, sending this form letter to their wives: "Your husband has got into the habit of staying out late of nights. I wish you would find out where he goes and what he does, and let me know."

Ben Chapman thought up a clever scheme of checking when he managed the Phillies. The elevator man who came on at midnight at the club's spring headquarters, the Fort Harrison Hotel in Clearwater, was a baseball bug. So Ben would give him a baseball and suggest that he get some of the Phillies' autographs before he went off duty at 8 A.M., and show him the ball the next night. Thus Chapman got the real evidence—in writing.

Of late St. Petersburg Beach has been a favorite spring training spot for writers. A colony sprang up there at Pat Sergi's cottages, and at his death gradually shifted to the Gulf Winds Villas. One of our neighbors was Lefty Gomez, just after he had left the Yankees and joined a sporting goods company. Gomez was required by the company to fill out certain forms in regard to his previous employment. In the space which asked, "Why did you leave your last

98

position?" Lefty filled in: "I no longer could get the side out."

Baseball . . . March . . . Florida—they lure me just as much now as they did with Red Lucas in 1931. That was the year Uncle Wilbert Robinson, manager of the Brooklyn Dodgers, forbade pitcher Pea Ridge Day to break into an Arkansas hog call after fanning a hitter for the third out in an inning, explaining: "A man has no right to be sillier than God made him."

One reason I'm so fond of spring baseball is that on gloomy days columns can be written two or three days in advance, with little chance of spoiling. Also, that an afternoon newspaper sports editor, so used to arising early each morning, can repose a bit, breakfasting at ten o'clock and not eating again until dinner.

This is as good a spot as any to advance my notion of a Lunchless Monday—or Tuesday or Wednesday or Thursday or Friday—based on the belief that seven-eighths of the people in the United States eat too much, and would be healthier and feel better if they skipped one meal a week.

Suppose just 100,000 adults in this country, principally business and professional men and women, agreed to forego lunch one day a week and instead threw the lunch money, say fifty cents, into a kitty?

That would be $2,600,000 a year.

But I don't know. The best use of the money I've saved by skipping lunch is to spend it on dinner and breakfast.

The Sign Says: "Baseball's
Most Historic Park"

Baseball, with its sun and fun (ever hear of anybody getting tired of batting practice?) had been my favorite game, and from the first days on a newspaper it was the sport I liked best to cover. The minor leagues, like the majors, were peopled with odd, entertaining characters and Nashville and the Southern Association always seemed to get their share.

Fact is, the Nashville ball park itself was—and is—good copy for every sportswriter seeing it for the first time. Arthur Daley, New York *Times* columnist, after a recent visit, remarked: "I've heard about it all my life and I still don't believe it."

Originally a trading, watering and picnic spot in pioneer days, the playing field is twenty-two feet below street level, occupying a downtown block near the Tennessee state capitol building. At no other plot of ground in America has baseball been played as long; there is a newspaper account of a game there in 1866, when it was known as Sulphur Springs

Bottom. Grantland Rice gave it the name Sulphur Dell when he wrote sports in Nashville. To Bobo Newsom, it looked like "a drained-out bathtub." There always has been a rightfield embankment, called the "dump," and the rightfield fence, topped with a high screen, is only 262 feet from home plate. Home run hitters develop an up-stroke; many Nashville batsmen have lifted 25 or more drives over the fence in a 77-game home schedule. When outfielder Bob Lennon, later with the New York Giants, set the Southern Association home run record in 1955, 40 of his 64 homers were hit in the Dell. Sometimes a man is thrown out at first base on a sharp blow to rightfield, while a tall, tall fly that caroms crazily off the fence can be run into a triple. A new right-fielder trying to patrol the incline provides fans much added amusement.

Heavy-footed Smead Jolley, a lumbering good-slug, no-field athlete, played the Nashville dump when it was steeper. One day he charged a hard-hit drive, which skipped past him, allowing the runner to reach second base, and as the ball rebounded from the fence it trickled through Jolley's legs, the runner going on to third. Then Smead threw over the catcher's head, the runner scoring, and only the official scorer's kindness robbed Jolley of the remarkable feat of three errors on one play.

Off the field, Jolley is remembered best as a hotel room poker player who would tear up the deck when the cards were running bad. One night a newspaperman kibitzing over Smead's shoulder as a stud pot grew bigger and bigger suddenly peeped at Jolley's hole card, then stepped to the telephone and called room service, saying: "Send up another deck, please."

Baseball used to have a language of its own, fascinating to a young sportswriter. Most of the players talked in the present tense and there was standard mispronouncing, or pluralizing, of proper names. A typical dugout monologue:

"I'm playing in Shrevesport this day, and I'm in the worst slump of my life. I can't buy a base hit. Them pitchers ain't got enough stuff to fan Rosie O'Grady, but me—I might as well be swinging with the *Sporting News*. If I do hit a line drive, them Bill Doaks (gloves) jump up like jimson weeds. But nobody daresn't kid me about it. I says to myself, 'If I don't get started, they're liable to send me to Wheeling.' This smart-aleck college kid says, 'Yeah, to wheeling dirt,' and—leave me tell you—I punch him!"

The game's true rowdies thrived long before my day, but Buster Brown, a Nashville first-baseman and pitcher of the 1920's, wouldn't have been out-toughed in any era. He was from East St. Louis and his nose and the tell-tale thickened scar-tissue beneath the skin around his eyes showed he had been a prize fighter. He carried a spring-lock knife with a blade about five inches long—actually kept it in his uniform— a fact well known to visiting players.

Regularly before a game Buster would stroll over to the visiting bench, stick his head in and ask, belligerently: "Any you guys want to fight?"

There would ensue a silence. Then Buster would say: "If you doesn't then keep your lip buttoned."

Brown could bite a chunk out of water glasses and chew it briskly. Sometimes the blood would come, and when Buster performed this act of humor in the cafes and corn whisky parlors, it would invariably cause any ladies present to scream, and maybe run, as The Buster pounded his knees in merriment and spit bloodily.

The Buster married one night in midsummer and the next afternoon the bride sat in the Sulphur Dell box seats, halfway down the first base line. She wore a man's cap and a gold tooth showed as she chewed away at her gum, rooting for bull-necked Buster to slam a home run. A wretched umpire called a strike on Buster which was disputed with heat. But The Buster calmed. "If it wasn't for that little lady sittin' over there," he said, gesturing nobly toward her, "I would bust you one."

In my first year of sportswriting, 1929, the Nashville manager was Clarence (Pants) Rowland—well-mannered, suave, the antithesis of toughness. He had played very little baseball (just a short time with Dubuque, Iowa, I think) yet managed the Chicago White Sox to the American League pennant in 1917 and beat the Giants in the World Series. He used to talk about how Heinie Zimmerman, the Giant third baseman, chased Eddie Collins across the plate with the first run of that last game of the '17 Series. "I ran right alongside Eddie," said Rowland, who had been coaching at third. "I told him later: 'You should have turned left at the plate and kept right on running to first base. He'd a-followed you all the way and Hap Felsch could have scored, too.'"

Rowland appeared self-conscious in a baseball uniform. He seemed much more at ease off the field, dapper, with his hat brim turned down on the side and slightly in the back, instead of in front. Now he has also been an umpire, scout and league president, and at seventy-six Rowland remains active in the Chicago Cubs' organization. In any capacity, Clarence is unlikely to re-experience his 1930 fate; on that Nashville club, first baseman Jim Poole poled 50 home runs, second baseman Jay Partridge hit 40, the team as a whole whammed 157, had a club batting average of .315, and scored 6.6 runs per game, yet finished seventh. Some pitching Rowland had!

Only baseball man I've known who equaled or surpassed Rowland's versatility was the late Billy Evans, a great umpire, the game's best authority on the rules, an intelligent writer and historian who served as farm director of the Boston Red Sox and general manager of the Detroit Tigers. As president of the Southern Association, Evans kept the league operating throughout World War II into the years of its greatest prosperity. But when I think of Billy, here is what is most apt to pop into my memory:

Attending a Nashville game one summer night, Evans first dined with friends and all rode to the ball park in the automobile of Slick Welsh, widely-known Southern clothier who in 1955 was chosen America's No. 1 sports fan. As Evans was getting out of the back seat, and talking, somehow the front door was slammed on his right hand, mashing his fingers. Billy groaned in pain and gritted his teeth, but was the perfect gentleman, declining medication and proceeding to the game. Afterward, returning to the same car to be driven to the railroad station, Billy re-entered the back seat, stuck his left paw—the good one—through the open window to grab a hold on the door frame and pull himself forward, and somebody slammed that door! Billy screamed, leapt from the car wringing his hand and fled into the darkness cursing his fate and Mr. Welsh's mobile torture chamber. Finally he took a cab to the station, first sticking both hands deep in his coat pockets. I doubt if any other person in the history of the world ever experienced such a billion-to-one double-slam.

When bad luck comes in concentrated doses, and the snakes are really after you, I'm reminded of Rod Murphy, an Atlanta first baseman in the 1920's. In a game at Nashville his first-inning error had permitted two runs. He popped up the first time at bat, struck out the next time and on the third trip, with runners on first and second and none out, he hit into a double play. Exasperated and self-condemning, Murphy chose not to return to the Atlanta bench, but exiled himself for the remainder of the inning by sitting on the ground against the grandstand wall in short right field. In the front row box seats at this exact location were two little boys whose doting father had over-stuffed them with peanuts, popcorn, ice cream and soft drinks. One became sick, in a big way, vomiting right on Mr. Murphy, and I can see Rod now, stalking to the clubhouse leaving cap and shirt behind and raving to heaven.

In the spring of 1930 I met Casey Stengel for the first time. He was managing Toledo of the American Association, training at Anniston, Alabama, and Nashville traveled there for an exhibition series. Then, as now, what impressed me most was Stengel's matchless feel for comic effect; what Casey said was funny, but the way he acted out something was funnier. One exaggerated little movement would give a vivid impersonation of some of his Toledo players, maybe Butch Henline, the chunky catcher, or Hugh McQuillan, one-time Giant pitcher and playboy, or Cowboy Jones, a gangling outfielder. His rendition of an old infielder named Dots Miller, a between-season fireman at Kearny, New Jersey, sliding down a pole, or his former manager at Brooklyn, rotund Wilbert Robinson, trying to get into a rubber girdle would almost make The Sphinx laugh out loud. Casey's rugged, wrinkled face usually had—and has—the look of a person confronted with grave problems; today he's difficult to visualize as the young outfielder at Maysville, Kentucky in the Bluegrass League in 1910 who used to practice hook slides when he went to and from his position, or as the big league batsman from whose head flew a sparrow when he tipped his cap to a razzing audience.

Stengel to me is the foremost example of baseball's unpredictability. At fifty-seven, he was just a former major leaguer managing in the minors, figured to be about through; greatness came to him in life's ninth inning.

The Nashville club in 1931, in one of the queer twists of the depression following the 1929 stock market crash, became the property of Hardeman County in rural West Tennessee through collateral forfeit by the Southern banking empire of Caldwell & Co. At a Federal Court sale the club's assets (real estate, franchise and players) were purchased by Bob Allen, a baseball veteran who had operated for many years at Little Rock. Mr. Allen had a reputation for thriftiness; they said he saved all incoming mail envelopes and made note pads therefrom. Also, that the most miserable experience of his life was when he chose a second-rate hotel at the 1926 baseball convention at Catalina Island only to discover, on the last day, that owner William Wrigley, Jr., had picked up the tab for all the baseball guests who stayed at his plush hostelry. However, all my relations with Mr. Allen and his sons, Bob, Jr., and Edgar were pleasant and my one and only baseball "discovery" (every sportswriter has at least one) launched his career with the Allens.

The box score of the opening game of the 1931 season has "Sewell, rf." in Nashville's lineup against Birmingham. His first name was Truett, fresh out of Vanderbilt University; the major leagues came to know him as Rip, winner of 143 games with Pittsburgh (1939-48) and inventor of the celebrated blooper pitch. The Allens farmed him to Raleigh, North Carolina, and when they sold the Nashville club to Fay Murray in June, 1931, the new owners didn't know Sewell belonged to them. They discovered it only when a telegram was received from Detroit one day in August asking how much they wanted for Sewell. The Nashville general manager, Jimmy Hamilton, rushed to Raleigh, where he found Rip playing outfield on the days he wasn't pitching and actually driving the team bus on trips. Detroit paid $10,000 for him. Sewell was ten years reaching his peak, one of many major league pitchers at their best at 33 and 35. At no other position does experience so offset the physical liabilities of age. Pitchers don't necessarily have to be athletes; some of the best couldn't run or hit and would have been awkward attempting another sport. Sewell, however, was an exception, being extremely well-coordinated. Off the field, he's perhaps remembered best as the player chiefly responsible for preventing a strike of Pittsburgh

106

Pirates an hour before game time on the night of June 7, 1946, persuading a sufficient number to vote against it.

Jimmy Hamilton, an Ohioan who managed all over the minors, including Nashville (1923-28), was notorious for always having three clubs: one coming, one going and one on the field. At Mobile in 1930 he traveled with twelve regular players and in each of the seven other Southern Association cities signed semipros for three-day stretches. Jimmy was unpredictable, a violent extremist, cordial one day and not speaking the next. During a Nashville road slump he threw all the bats off the train, proclaiming that to pay freight on them was sheer waste. He detested the wearing of knickers and once made two players change to overalls, saying they "should be learning a trade." At other times he might be jovial, especially if some big league "has-been" he had signed, like Flint Rhem or Kent Greenfield or Fred Toney, arrived in time to be billed as Sunday's pitcher and thus swell the crowd a few hundred. Jimmy scouted all over the lower minors, and he delighted in fabricating outlandish experiences. "I was up in the Middle Atlantic League last summer," he would say. "They opened in April and they have twelve clubs. It's now August and I ask this room clerk in the hotel at Youngstown, 'How does the Beckley club look?' He said, 'I don't know, sir; they ain't played here yet.'"

Hamilton was an exceptionally good judge of baseball talent. I think the late Kiki Cuyler, outfielder who played under him at Nashville, was the best all-round minor leaguer I ever saw. And on a look-back basis, perhaps the most underrated major league player of his time. Through fifteen seasons with Pittsburgh, the Chicago Cubs, Cincinnati and Brooklyn, Cuyler's lifetime major league batting average was .321; in 1929 he hit .360, the next year .355. Three years he led the league in games played, four years in stolen

107

bases, twice in runs scored, often in triples and doubles. Average-wise he ranks with Harry Heilmann, Rogers Hornsby, Jimmy Foxx, Hank Greenberg and Joe DiMaggio as one of the best of the right-hand hitters. And with his arm, how Cuyler used to "shoot" runners out at the plate, trying to score from third base after he caught a fly! Baseball of today may be better in many respects, but outfielders' throwing arms aren't among its proofs of superiority.

The Nashville club owner, Fay Murray, who died in 1941, was the kind of "angel" every minor league city dreams of having—wealthy, generous, baseball his hobby and with excellent major league connections. Due to his friendship with Bill Terry, Nashville first worked with the Giants; later, he allied with former Nashville resident Larry MacPhail at both Cincinnati and Brooklyn. Had Murray lived, I'm confident he would have joined MacPhail as one of the purchasers of the New York Yankees in 1945.

Strangest bargain I've witnessed in baseball resulted in Charlie Dressen, jobless and broke, getting his first chance as a manager at Nashville in July, 1932.

"How do I know you can manage?" Murray asked him.

Dressen had no ready answer for that, but inquired as to what would be expected for the remainder of the season.

"I want a team that can beat .500, can win over half its games," Murray explained. "That's all I ask this year. We got off to a bad start; we've won 36 and lost 40 now. I won't have a manager who can't win more than half his games."

"Here's a proposition," Dressen said. "Make me manager the rest of the season and if the club doesn't win over half its games, you don't owe me a cent of salary. Just bare expenses."

Murray, amused, took him up. On the last day of the season, Nashville under Dressen had won exactly 38 games and lost 38. That afternoon they broke loose for a six-run rally in the eighth inning to win the final game from Atlanta, 12 to 8. And a manager had started on his way to the big leagues.

Cocky Charlie, a bantam with unlimited confidence, wouldn't have made it as fast as he did but for Bill Terry's selflessness. As 1933 New York Giants' manager, Terry summoned Dressen as a reserve infielder at the tail-end of the season when appendicitis sidelined third baseman Johnny Vergez. In the World Series with Washington, the last half of the eleventh inning of the fourth game found the Giants leading 2 to 1 behind Carl Hubbell with the bases full and only one out. Cliff Bolton, hard-hitting catcher, who had played at Chattanooga, came up as a pinch-hitter for Washington. Terry called time, gathered his infield around the pitcher's mound and instructed them to play in on the grass to try to cut the run off at the plate.

Without being asked, Dressen dashed from the dugout and told Terry: "You're playing Bolton wrong, Bill. Put your infield back and pitch him high and outside. He hits down on a ball, and he's slow."

Hesitantly, Terry changed. Bolton hit a scorching grounder to Blondy Ryan at shortstop to start a double play and the game was over.

Afterward, Terry gave Dressen full credit. "That's what helped me so much," Charlie said. "Some managers would never have bothered to mention the conversation that went on out there on the mound."

More Of Baseball's Peculiar Drollery

Someone has said that baseball enjoys its present stature in the American mind because people succumbed to the magic of green grass in an enclosed park, bat against oncoming ball, speed against throwing—skill in action. Which is largely true. Baseball is easy for the spectator to understand. It's free of the aura of mystery which the rules-makers and the coaches give to football and basketball.

The distance from home plate to first, and between the bases, is exactly the same as when Abner Doubleday or Alexander Cartwright or some never to be known architect invented the game. How did this genius figure ninety feet was the precise balance for plays where the runner usually is out or safe by a bare step? How was it finally determined that pitcher's box at sixty feet and six inches from home plate presented the sharpest measure of competition between pitcher and hitter?

Fascinating scientific precision and fetching simplicity are the broad beams of baseball's stage. But the "actors" make the game what it is in the major and minor leagues. Roy Campanella, veteran Brooklyn catcher, said recently:

110

"You have to be a man to be a professional ball player, but you have to have a lot of little boy in you, too." It's a business to these adults who work in short pants and caps, but to most of them it's also fun. Baseball through the years developed a sort of humor of its own. I think the main reason it flourished was because the players had so much time on their hands. Besides the hours and hours to while away at hotels on road trips, time often hangs heavy on the players when they're not in the game—the utility men and the extra pitchers and catchers.

A newspaperman once asked Johnny Gooch, a long-time National Leaguer with Pittsburgh, Brooklyn and Cincinnati before he came back to the minors: "Of what feat are you proudest?" Gooch answered: "I've got nothing to be proud of; I'm a catcher." Gooch was the best catcher I ever saw at blocking a runner off home plate, but he stands out in my memory more as one of the funniest practitioners of baseball's peculiar drollery. When a rookie on the 1935 Nashville club stole third base in a rousing slide only to find a teammate perched there, the dugout crackled with bitter condemnation of such a bonehead play. All except Gooch, who commented calmly: "In the boy's favor, I must say he did have a big lead."

Almost every day Johnny unfolded some wild tale to swear to as an eye-witnessed happening. He claimed to have seen a semipro game wherein a batsman hit a seven-bagger. ("The ball went over the center-fielder's head, the hitter circled the bases only to be told he hadn't touched second, so he started out again and made it all the way to third before they got the ball back to the infield.")

Gooch reported to spring training one year telling about an ice hockey game he had attended during the winter. "Roughest stuff I ever saw," he said. "Two guys are fighting over a little piece of wood that they push around over the ice. One fellow runs up and bashes the other over the

111

head with a stick. The guy drops like he's shot. The umpire or whatever you call him skates up, takes out his watch, stands over this fellow who's stretched out there on the ice and says: 'I'll give you two minutes to get up and play.' And you know how long that guy was out? Eleven weeks!"

One time during a minor league baseball convention Johnny pointed across the crowded hotel lobby and said: "Over yonder is one of the smartest men in the history of baseball." I looked, trying to spot Branch Rickey or George Weiss or some other master-mind, to no avail, when Gooch identified one of his old catching brethren. "He got a job last year as business manager of a club up East," Johnny explained. "Messed up the books so they had to hire him back."

Now out of baseball, Gooch often exercises a mock cynicism. I saw him in Nashville one day recently thumbing a ride in the opposite direction from which all traffic was moving. "Just trying to spot a true friend," he said. "A true friend is one who'll turn his car around and take you where you want to go."

I was sitting next to him at a cafe counter one time when he had trouble getting salt to come out of the shaker. "Don't nothing work no more," he said.

Among Gooch's many lasting friends is Johnny Vander Meer, only man in baseball history to pitch two consecutive no-hit games. (For Cincinnati against Boston, June 11, and against Brooklyn, June 15, 1938.) Vander Meer failed with Nashville in the spring of 1936 due to wildness, and was farmed to Durham, North Carolina, in the Piedmont League, where Gooch was manager. Gooch decided the left-handed fastballer wasn't stepping toward the plate, so one midnight by lantern light he and Charles Hunter, Negro clubhouse boy, moved the Durham pitching rubber a few inches to the right. The first hitter Vander Meer faced the next game banged a home run off him, but he continued to get the

112

ball over the plate, winning 19 games that season and striking out 295.

Many catchers become managers. Among the four now handling major league clubs is Paul Richards of Baltimore, intelligent, highly imaginative and—in his days at Atlanta—the owner of a fiery temper. During one season, 1938, umpires ejected him twenty-three times. When his club wasn't playing to suit him, Richards enforced a rule that nobody could take a shower until the manager did. If he sat and brooded for an hour after a defeat, the players had to sit and brood too.

The maddest I ever saw Richards was during a game in late August, 1941, when Atlanta and Nashville were battling down the wire for the pennant. With two outs in the eighth inning and the score tied 1 to 1, a Nashville runner, shortstop Dick Culler, had reached third base. Just as Atlanta pitcher Emil Lochbaum was in the middle of his windup, Culler yelled "Time! Time!" Thinking it was the third-base umpire hollering, Lochbaum suddenly stopped, committing a balk, and Culler walked over with what was to be the winning run. The Atlanta players remained in the clubhouse most of the night listening to Richards rage.

Richards seldom criticized his players openly, but his sarcasm could be devastating. One day the Atlanta catcher, Spec Dozier, pegged the ball into centerfield attempting to throw out a runner stealing second. "My fault, gang! My fault!" bellowed Dozier. When he came back to the bench at the end of the inning, Richards said, icily: "Dozier, every so-and-so in the park knows it was your fault. I don't see much point in reminding them."

A slice of Paul's roughly picturesque language I remember is this advice to his young players: "Never be meek or morose, no matter how many times you get beat. Go out there ferocious, like a bitin' sow."

What I would like to see Richards do some day, perhaps

by way of exhibiting his "ambidextrousness" for the dual role of Baltimore general manager-field manager, would be go to the pitcher's mound and throw both ways. He used to be a pitcher, once winning a doubleheader for Waxahachie, Texas, high school by throwing right-handed to right-handed batters and left-handed to left-handed batters. Later, with Muskogee, Oklahoma of the Western Association, he baffled Topeka batters the same way until a switch-hitter, Charlie Wilson, came up in the ninth inning to pinch-hit. Wilson moved from one side of the plate to the other, trumping Paul's similar shifts, until—"Finally," Richard says, "I threw my glove down on the ground, faced him square with both feet on the rubber, put my hands behind my back, and let him choose his own poison."

Richards was never a wisecracker. One of the champions in this department is Lafayette (Fresco) Thompson, vice-president in charge of the Brooklyn Dodgers' farm clubs, who also served in the Southern Association as manager at Birmingham and New Orleans. But the first time I saw Fresco he was a utility infielder with the Giants, passing through Nashville for an exhibition. Late in the game, Frank Snyder, coaching at first, told Thompson to go in as a pinch-runner. "Thank you, Frank," he said, "but I've just had my shoes shined." Very shortly thereafter, Thompson was through as a major-leaguer.

As Birmingham manager Fresco coached at third base and, when irritated beyond the legal limit by a persistent heckler, would go over and inquire the name of the man's undertaker. "I want your head," he would say, "for my rock garden."

Thompson had Birmingham in the thick of the pennant race in 1938, but the club slumped, and I suppose it was the sight of the gay one in a fretful mood which prompted a delicate gag at his expense on a hot night in Nashville

114

near the end of the season. A goodly crowd was on hand, and behind the plate was a fat, noticeably nervous young umpire freshly promoted from the Southeastern League.

Although Birmingham grabbed an early lead, it didn't keep Thompson from riding the new umpire from the very first inning. He would sit on the concrete steps of the visiting club's dugout and direct a steady flow of uncomplimentary remarks which could be heard plainly up in the press box.

The idea occurred that Fresco should be sent a note, so a dainty missive was written in feminine backhand style and dispatched via the press box messenger boy who in delivering it remarked that "a lady back there in the box seats said to give this to you." It read:

"Dear Mr. Thompson: I drove all the way from Dothan, Alabama, today to see my nephew umpire his first Southern League game and I will appreciate it very much if you will quit saying such ugly things to him.
                    LOU ELLA BROWN."

After reading the note, Fresco folded it up, put it in his hip pocket, and immediately ceased his banter. For almost three innings, he said nothing to the umpire.

Came the seventh, and Nashville put on a rally, going one run ahead. Birmingham came back the next round and had runners on first and second with none out, but on a single to centerfield the runner on second was thrown out on a very close play at the plate.

The player, jumping up in a cloud of dust as the umpire signaled him out, protested so that he was ejected from the game. Thompson raved and ranted, kicked dirt over home plate, all but pushed the new umpire, making quite a scene and barely escaping being chased. When he finally returned to his seat on the steps, his abuse of the umpire was worse than ever. Surely Fresco had forgotten about the umpire's dear old "aunt" up in the stands, who had driven over 450 miles for this occasion.

It was time to send another note.

In the same handwriting, and delivered by the same boy, the message went on its way. As Thompson received and unfolded same, it read:

"Mr. Thompson: If you don't stop insulting my nephew, I'm going to come down there and kick you in the (censored). LOU ELLA BROWN."

Fresco rolled right off the top step and hit smack on the ground. He stayed there flat on his back until players rushed from the Birmingham dugout and lifted him, brushing off his uniform and asking if he wanted a doctor. He said nothing, just handed them the note.

They read it and seemed to understand what a shock it had been for their manager.

For the rest of the season and on into the winter Fresco was telling about this strange experience, of what an impulsive, bitterly outspoken lady fan he had encountered, and it wasn't until three years later that a confession was made to him.

When Thompson moved to New Orleans as manager, one of his pet annoyances was the detailed report he had to make for the parent Brooklyn club. He knew that Branch Rickey disliked generalities, that he demanded specific analyses of young players' strong and weak points. One day Fresco reported as follows on a young pitcher: "This boy is wild low. He doesn't have enough stuff to be wild high."

Luckily, Thompson had left New Orleans before the advent of catcher Del Ballinger, who might have threatened to move in on his fun-some domain. Ballinger once "shot" an umpire. It happened at Oakland when Del was catching for San Diego. Before the game he and Pepper Martin, then managing San Diego, had noticed that the clubhouse boy had a toy pistol that looked like the real thing, so they borrowed it, Del sticking it in his hip pocket.

The game reached the eighth inning with San Diego behind, 15 to 1. They had been playing two hours and fifty minutes. Ballinger had a sore thumb and throughout the game had been taking his time calling the pitches, much to the umpire's annoyance. Then Del called time out and began to rub his thumb and seemed to be wasting more time. The umpire told Ballinger that if he didn't quit taking so much time he was going to put him out, and possibly forfeit the game.

"If you mess with me, I'll shoot you," Ballinger said, looking wild-eyed.

After the next pitch, a strike, Del called time.

"What in the world's the matter with you?" the umpire asked. "You're behind 15 to 1, we've been playing three hours, and you call time. I oughta' throw you out!"

Never cracking a smile, Ballinger reached into his hip pocket for the gun and stuck it in the umpire's stomach. The ump began backing up to the screen behind home plate. Then, as he began to look in both directions, trying to pick out which way to run, Del pulled the trigger. The pistol popped and smoke came out. The umpire staggered, but couldn't find any blood, then regained his balance quickly enough to order the prankster from the game.

In later years Ballinger was satisfied with milder tricks, such as sewing a dark green string into a baseball—and also into his mitt. At certain intervals when catching he would slip this ball from his pocket and throw it back toward the pitcher, but wild enough for it to roll toward the base umpire. As the umpire would reach for it, Del would jerk the string and the ball would dart back toward the plate, making the umpire feel—and look—just a bit silly.

Another funster to reform before he arrived in the

Southern Association as Nashville manager in 1949 was Rollie Hemsley. A pennant winner his first year, too. When Rollie was catching for the St. Louis Browns, he used to bring in a basket of frogs from his farm and distribute one to a berth in the railroad sleeper as a road trip began. Manager Rogers Hornsby fined him $50. "Hornsby was against playing cards, drinking beer and almost anything else you can think of," Hemsley said. "So one night before we left on a trip, I bought a knitting set, got a corner seat in the smoker and pretended to knit. Wasn't doing too bad, either. When Hornsby came around, he fined me $150. I bet I'm the only ball player in history who ever got fined for knitting."

Hornsby spent part of the 1938 season in the Southern Association as Chattanooga manager under Joe Engel, warmhearted extrovert who has operated that club since 1929. Joe prompted his wife, Hallie, that Mr. Hornsby was a major-leaguer unused to the "bushes" and to do her best to try to make him feel at home. At dinner on the evening of his arrival, Mrs. Engel's first remark was: "Well, Mr. Hornsby, how do you like it down here in the switches?"

Later that season Engel presented an aged, spindly horse and a long-billed jockey cap to Hornsby in a home plate ceremony which accented The Rajah's past addiction for playing the races, displeasing mightily the high commissioner of baseball, Judge Kenesaw Mountain Landis. But who could get mad at Joe Engel? He gets the happiest mileage out of life of anybody I know in sports, because he can make people laugh, and laugh himself, and laugh *AT* himself. Yes, even when a jockey riding one of his race horses, Hallieboy, was caught using a battery and a newspaperman wired Joe:

"Would appreciate some of your future business. (Signed) GENERAL ELECTRIC."

Engel was a Washington pitcher in his youth, noted in the American League mainly for his wildness—on and off the

118

field. But Joe was Clark Griffith's favorite and he more than justified the Old Fox's affection, understanding and confidence by developing into a shrewd baseball scout who acquired for the Washington club such gems as Joe Cronin, Bucky Harris, Buddy Myer, Goose Goslin, Joe Kuhel, Cecil Travis, Buddy Lewis and dozens of others. A former off-season vaudevillian in an act with baseball comedians Nick Altrock and Al Schacht, florid Engel is a natural showman who believes that fans paying their way into a ball park are in a mood for fun. On this theory, plus a keen sense of customers' appreciation of cleanliness and comfort, he has held forth in Class AA baseball for almost thirty years in a city whose population ranged from only 100,000 to 135,000.

On an April morning in 1938, fierce-sounding elephantine roars and growls brought Chattanoogans out of their homes and stores to discover three tightly-closed trucks, with straw sticking out, en route to the ball park. Guards with guns permitted no one near the "animals." A newspaper story announced all Chattanooga ballplayers had been vaccinated for jungle fever, for that afternoon's game opening the season would feature a gigantic elephant hunt. More than 15,000 turned out to see scantily-clad Negroes with spears dash out of grass huts yelling cannibal-like and join armed hunters (on wooden horses) in stalking their prey. The cloth pachyderms died horribly.

Engel has staged innumerable other stunts, putting singing canaries in the grandstand to soothe the fans when the club was going bad; signing a girl pitcher who "struck out" both Babe Ruth and Lou Gehrig in an exhibition game; hiring an Indian ballplayer and later "scalping" him, thus avenging General Custer, etc., etc. Yet it's off the field that Engel enlivens things even more so by exploiting every gag possibility.

At a Chattanooga game he happened to spot umpires Buck Campbell and Claude Bond sitting in the grandstand. They explained they had been scheduled to work in Nashville, but en route had been advised that the game there had been postponed, so had stopped over for a busman's holiday. Engel promptly framed the scoreboard boy to hang up a first-inning score of the Nashville game just as if it were being played, resulting in the umpires going into a quick and worried huddle and rushing to the long distance telephone.

Chattanooga once had a working agreement with the Selma, Alabama, club, operated by Engel's bosom friend, the late Maurice Bloch. One morning Engel telephoned Bloch that he was forced to recall immediately Johnny Burrows, pitching ace of the Selma staff. After being convinced it was no joke, the infuriated Bloch sputtered: "All right, I'll send back your pitcher. But I want you to know this ends our friendship, forever. Never speak to me again. And I hope I never lay eyes on you." When Bloch arrived home for lunch, he found on his front porch three tons of ice and a telegram which read: "Just something to cool you off. Love, Joe."

A player Engel was trying to sign for Chattanooga one season wired him: "Double the salary or count me out." The next day he received this telegram from Joe: "1, 2, 3, 4, 5, 6, 7, 8, 9, 10."

A new radio broadcaster of Chattanooga games confided to park employees his concern over Engel's high excitement and apparent surge in blood pressure during tense moments of play. Shortly thereafter, the announcer glanced from his microphone during a Chattanooga rally to see Joe (who had slipped Bromo-Seltzer into his mouth), mumbling and foaming. The announcer rushed out of his booth and before Engel could make his getaway, emptied a bucket of water on him.

On another occasion when Engel was left speechless, he wasn't trying to be funny. Chattanooga had lost a game in the ninth inning when veteran pitcher Clyde Barfoot threw a change of pace which an opposing hitter clobbered for a home run. Joe awaited Barfoot outside the dressing room and approached him, asking: "Why in the world, Clyde, did you throw a change of pace to that fellow?" Barfoot looked him straight in the eye and replied coldly: "Because it was in my repertoire."

When Engel was trying to sell outfielder Bill Nicholson to the Chicago Cubs, he arranged for ladened little boys to enter his office and interrupt conversations with Jack Doyle, wizened old Cub scout, saying: "Mr. Engel, here are some more balls that Nicholson hit over the fence yesterday." Which would make the knowing Doyle boom and curse, but he paid $40,000 for Nicholson, even after complaining that the mint juleps hospitable Mrs. Engel served him needed "more grass and less whisky."

Until recently, Engel himself was a seldom outdistanced drinker. Yet he would show more morning-after sparkle and zest than any convivialist I've known. Joe's favorite breakfast used to be six or eight gin fizzes made with whites of eggs. "Must have my eggs for breakfast," he would explain, huskily.

"I figure I've crowded about 180 years into my life," Joe says. "In my will, I've requested that my funeral be held at home plate in my ball park, then carry me to deep centerfield and bury me there as a band plays 'Please Don't Talk About Me When I'm Gone.'"

Only baseball devotional I know of to approach Joe Engel's came from Gus Jebeles when he owned the Birmingham club. A native of Greece, Mr. Jebeles preferred to remain in the background at public functions and let the club's general manager, Paul Florence, make the speeches. But one day at a civic luncheon Jeb nudged Paul and whispered that he would like to be called on for a few words. As he arose, everybody wondered what the shy Greek would say.

"Since little boy, always like baseball," Jeb began, in his engaging dialect. "One time I'm playing on street with my two brothers. Man come by. He stop, say to my oldest brother: 'Sam, what you rather have than anything in world?' Sam say: 'Money.'

"Then to my other brother he say: 'Charlie, what you rather have than anything in world?' Charlie say: 'Rather have automobile.'

"Then he turn to me and say: 'Gus, what you rather have?' I say I rather have third eye than anything in world.

"He wanna' know why I want third eye. I tell him: 'So I can put it on end of stick, push stick through knothole, and see ball game.' "

Let Me Tell You About Larry

The most extraordinary person I've known in sports is
Larry Gilbert. In twenty-five years as a manager, first at
New Orleans (1923-1938) and then at Nashville (1939-
1948), he was out of the first division three times, the best
long-distance record in baseball. His teams won nine pen-
nants. He turned down six chances to manage in the major
leagues because (1) he liked the South and (2) he was
making all the money he needed.

Larry Gilbert is an almost legendary figure, not because
of his baseball success but because of the kind of man he
was. Principles and honorable practices sometimes seem to
sag with the quickening world pace and its increasing
complexities; baseball has its sharp dealings, and in an
industry so dependent upon goodwill and publicity there
are temptations to dodge questions, withhold facts or twist
an angle. But Larry didn't know how to speak anything
but the truth.

Until proved otherwise, to him every person was on the
up-and-up. That, despite rumors or reputation. He made
allowances for human frailties. Larry's idea of an even break

123

was to give every other person a slight edge. Yet he was no turn-the-other-cheek man; if pushed around, he could unload—purply.

What continues to amaze his friends is that Gilbert was raised in one of the toughest environments, the "Irish Channel" section of New Orleans. But about him there was a native goodness which expressed itself throughout his life.

Simple, every-day happenings revealed his built-in kindness. There's no telling how much money he has given away just at ball park gates, clubhouse doors and on the street. Any down-and-outer could touch him. Many an uninvited youngster of little or no baseball ability showed up at his training camps, spent all his money and had no way to get home. Larry was always good for bus fare.

I remember when one of his former Nashville players, often in a jam, his career now over, lost his job and wrote Gilbert that he just had to have $100 for thirty days. Larry sent it.

"You know you'll never get that back, don't you?" said an office associate.

"That's all right," Larry answered. "He played mighty good ball for me, better than I expected. Maybe I owe him a little something."

On trips, walk down a city street with Larry and he would buy a paper from every old man and little boy hawker, then toss all but one away before he got back to his hotel. Why? "Aw, I just want to help their business," he would explain, embarrassed.

Larry seemed to arise each day with renewed thanksgiving for life and health and happiness, and he demonstrated it in little acts of generosity. He made a good living out of baseball and he was grateful. (He's now retired, living on the shore of Lake Ponchartrain at New Orleans.) Naturally such qualities contributed to his managerial suc-

124

cess. Players who advanced from his early training to the major leagues sent their brothers and their friends' sons and brothers to Larry.

Managing a ball club, his formula was simple: "Make winning so pleasant, and losing so unpleasant, that hustle is automatic."

Larry operated on the basis that there was a time for horseplay and a time for being serious. At the start of a season, almost anything went with him. There were no strict training rules. Players could come in at any reasonable hour of night. They could take a drink. No questions were asked as long as they were fit for play and the club won its share of games. But let them go into a losing streak, and the rainbow could flare into a tornado. Gilbert could be rough in his language, sparing no player suspected of giving less than 101 per cent. A victory, and all would be sweetness and light again, with Larry the happiest, kiddingest fellow around.

It's generally agreed that Gilbert had more success handling problem players than any man in baseball. Their reputation as screwballs or bad actors or drinkers didn't faze him. At New Orleans in 1938 he traded for a pitcher named Red Evans, who promised Larry to be in shape every fourth day if Larry would let him sit up in the Negro bleachers and "have fun" each day after he pitched, "announcing" the game with a megaphone a la Red Barber. On that plan, Evans won twenty-one games and was voted the Southern Association's most valuable player. Another pitcher, Earl Hilton, prospered on the privilege of being allowed $1 extra each day to play slot machines.

After moving to Nashville, Gilbert sought the well-known zany, Cletus Elwood (Boots) Poffenberger, then on Brooklyn's ineligible list. Poffenberger would take on any challenger in beer-drinking bouts, conducted on the basis of the first man who went to the men's room having to pay for all the beers. Suds and all, Poffenberger won twenty-nine games for Nashville in 1940.

One drinker, a rookie from the Florida State League, went a little too far with Larry, hiding his concoction of gin and paregoric in the dugout water cooler. Said the groundskeeper who discovered it: "Tastes like brimstone."

Gilbert sent seventy players to the major leagues. He made the Boston Braves take pitcher Johnny Sain on a "just-pay-me-when-you-get-the-money" agreement. Boldly, he changed Jack Harshman, now of the Chicago White Sox, into a pitcher after a season in which he hit forty-seven home runs as a first baseman. Larry felt he struck out too much. That year, 1951, Jack also drove in 141 runs while getting only 136 hits, which I claim must be an all-time record. In his first full season of pitching Harshman won twenty-three games for Nashville; he won forty in his first three seasons with the White Sox. Gilbert peddled catcher Greek George three separate times, for cash, to Cleveland, Brooklyn and the Chicago Cubs; Steve O'Neill, then Leo Durocher, then Jimmy Wilson banished George because he persisted in comparing them unfavorably with his previous manager, spouting: "Gilbert wouldn't play it that way." Incidentally, George was hepped on a fruit and vegetable diet, often going on fasts when he ate only grapes over a four-day stretch.

Outfielder Dusty Rhodes of the New York Giants was a Gilbert discovery, raised on a farm near Montgomery, Alabama. Nashville started him with Hopkinsville, Kentucky, in the Kitty League, where he was encountered walking toward the ball park one day eating a slice of bread with the rest of the loaf under his arm. "I had to eat cornbread all my life," Dusty explained. "I always said that if I got into baseball and got enough money I would buy a loaf of light bread and eat it all."

126

Larry knew how to handle every type. He had come up the hard way, and had made himself into an outstanding player, getting to the big leagues with the Boston Braves as a centerfielder and appearing in seventy-two games with their 1914 miracle club. Gilbert's insight, judgment and mental capacities, despite his limited school education, are reflected in his memory for detail and his articulate analysis of the Braves' unparalleled dash to the pennant, disclosing some facts little known today.

(Indeed, there actually might be a sports columnist somewhere in this favored land who never, never has written a July 4th column about the 1914 Braves.)

"Everybody knows that the Braves came from last place on July 4th to win the pennant, but we weren't just last—we were four games behind the seventh place club, Philadelphia," Gilbert recalled.

"To make it worse, we went to Buffalo on July 5th to play an exhibition and those International Leaguers beat us, 7 to 1.

"We started winning July 6th, a doubleheader from Brooklyn. From that date to the end of the season, we won 68 and lost only 20, a percentage of .773. The thing not to forget is that the 1914 Braves didn't just win the pennant, they won it by ten-and-a-half games.

"On into the World Series, winning those four straight from the Athletics, there never has been any three-man pitching like Tyler, Rudolph and James. And our manager, George Stallings, had a lot to do with them becoming winning pitchers the last half of the season. He did something I've never seen before or since by a manager.

"Stallings could stand almost anything but bases on balls. They drove him crazy. There was a time when James was so wild he couldn't last two or three innings. Tyler was inclined to be wild, too. Well, Stallings rode them so hard about bases on balls that he would go wild on the bench any time they got the count 2-2 on a hitter. He would curse them and rave. Even when they got the hitter out, he would ride them for not getting those two pitches over the plate. Stallings had sold himself on the belief that even in batting practice when a hitter knows the pitches are coming over the plate with nothing on them, odds are he will foul off a couple, bounce some more to the infield and lift two or three flies.

"I was on the bench most of the time, getting in as a pinch-hitter some, and sitting there day after day, I began to realize Stallings' tactics. In his own mind, and in his pitchers' minds, he simply made the 2-2 count as bad, as fatal, as walking a man. What Stallings did was just move up the 'danger stage' one pitch. He harped on that so much during the stretch drive that the pitchers were always trying to get the first ball across the plate. If not the first one, then the second one for sure. It changed a fair trio into a great trio."

There was a fourth Braves' pitcher, fun-loving Hub Perdue, who found Stallings' scalding tongue more than he could take and in midseason asked to be traded. Boston swapped him to St. Louis for outfielder George Whitted. Every time Gilbert sees Perdue, now a Tennessee farmer near Gallatin, he ribs him: "What did you get out of the World Series, Hub?"

"I got smart," Hub says.

After the one season with the Braves, when Larry dropped back to the minors and home, the New Orleans club for many years maintained a working agreement with Cleveland. Now that Bob Feller has retired, Gilbert reveals an insider's viewpoint on the famous Feller case which was before the baseball commissioner, Judge Landis, in 1936. Cleveland had signed Feller in July, 1935, and assigned him for 1936 service to Fargo-Moorhead of the Northern League. He refused to go there and was shifted to the New Orleans club, managed by Gilbert. Feller also refused to report to New Orleans, so in the summer of 1936 he was brought to Cleveland to work out with the Indians when the club was at home.

Lee Keyser, owner of the Des Moines club, complained that Feller, a farm boy from Van Meter, Iowa, had been working out in the Des Moines park and had been "stolen" and signed by Cleveland in violation of the major-minor agreement (no longer in effect) which prohibited a major league club from dealing with a sandlot player.

It was the most celebrated "free agency" case in baseball history. Feller, only seventeen, was being hailed as a second Walter Johnson. If taken away from Cleveland, his services would be open to the highest bidder. Most baseball people thought Landis, who took a delight in uncovering violations of baseball law and in punishing club owners, would declare Feller a free agent. That's what Gilbert thought when he was summoned to Chicago as a key witness.

The records in the case showed that the Cleveland club July 5, 1936, had sent a telegram to Gilbert asking his "permission" to use Feller in an exhibition game against the St. Louis Cardinals the next day. New Orleans "owned" Feller's contract; he was on that club's "voluntarily retired" list. Though Gilbert had never laid eyes on Feller, he wired his permission. The next day Bob pitched three innings and struck out eight of the nine Cardinals that faced him.

If Feller was a prize as an amateur, this made him the most sought-after youngster in baseball—if Landis freed him.

"Judge Landis throughout the proceedings gave Feller every possible opening to get his free agency," Gilbert said. "Landis surely knew Feller had not signed with Fargo-Moorhead, but had been signed directly for Cleveland by its scout, Cy Slapnicka. But Feller himself kept repeating to Landis that he wanted to be with Cleveland, that he wasn't seeking his free agency. I was impressed; the boy seemed to

129

feel that by signing his name he had obligated himself, and he wasn't thinking of the chance to get extra money.

"One of the funniest happenings of the case came when Judge Landis stuck his finger in Feller's face and asked why he didn't fulfill his intention of signing with Des Moines. 'Because,' Feller said, 'the groundskeeper told me Mr. Keyser was a cheap ——— —— — ———.' With that Keyser leaped up and shouted, 'That ——— —— — ——— is fired.'"

With a fondness for humor and a sense of what was "writeable," Gilbert was a newspaperman's dream. He used to keep a set of numbered alibis in the hip pocket of his uniform, and a player attempting to explain a misplay was stopped cold with the question, "What number this time?" He finally abandoned it after his centerfielder dropped a fly ball and sprang a brand new excuse: "A drop of rain got in my eye."

Gilbert's love of a gag even extended to the umpires. Two patriarchal arbiters in the Southern, Bill Brennan and Steamboat Johnson, each was bitterly jealous of his rank with the league president. After an unfavorable decision from Brennan, Gilbert's invariable parting sally was: "No wonder Johnson was made chief of staff." And vice versa.

For many years Larry carried as his New Orleans' second-string catcher a boyhood pal, Bob Dowie. One Sunday afternoon before an overflow crowd, with the score tied in the last of the ninth inning and the bases filled, Larry sent Dowie up as a pinch-hitter. The crowd booed loud—and then louder.

Calling time, Gilbert walked toward the plate, beckoning Dowie. He put his arm around Bob, saying: "Don't mind all this booing——"

"Hell, they ain't booing me, they're booing you for sending me up here," Dowie said. "They know I can't hit."

130

"I didn't send you up here to hit," Gilbert snapped. "I sent you up here to get hit."

Dowie followed instructions and the game was won.

I had thousands of happy hours with Gilbert, covering his teams. His favorite time was sundown, and a spot of bourbon, and friends. He had a rare warmth of spirit. I came to understand why two New Orleans sports editors actually cried when Larry left there for Nashville. There'll never be another like him.

Golf Is A Bedeviling Game, But—

Golf is a game in which I hold two distinctions: (1) I play my irons right-handed and my woods left-handed; (2) no partner or opponent, in thirty years, has ever asked me, "What club did you use on that shot?"

It's barely possible, of course, that the first peculiarity may explain the second. A golfing split personality, the agonizing outgrowth of right-handed throwing and left-handed batting, won't split many fairways—or hit many greens.

For a newspaperman, the happier side of golf is that it's so easy to cover. Compared with other sports, few people are involved. In match play finals, there are just two; in the last round—the payoff round—of medal play, usually only three or four pros are in the picture. More important, golfers are willing to talk about their game whether it has been good or bad, and they have amazingly accurate recollection for the graphic details.

I first discovered this in 1931. Our opposition newspaper in Nashville had the foresight and enterprise to send its sports editor to cover the Southern intercollegiate golf tournament at Athens, Georgia. We didn't think much about it until Albert Wheeler, a Vanderbilt student and Nashville boy, reached the semifinals. Wheeler won his match and entered the 36-hole Saturday finals for the championship. I got in touch with him by phone, and overnight he became our special correspondent doing his own by-lined, exclusive feature story of the match. During play, he didn't take a note, naturally; just telephoned (after he had won) and gave from memory a stroke-by-stroke account from first tee to last putt.

I've had many a football and baseball and basketball player tell me, immediately following a game, that they honestly didn't know exactly what happened on a decisive play, although they were in the thick of the action. But never a golfer; the golfer knows because he's concentrating so intently, and because his only opponent happens to be himself. A normal human being is more interested in himself than in anyone—or anything—else.

I'm sure Dr. Cary Middlecoff, holder of two National Open titles and a Master's crown, could replay every hole of the first tournament he won, the Tennessee State Amateur at Belle Meade Club in Nashville in 1937. Of all the top golfers I've known and followed, I believe Middlecoff is the most affected by mental attitude. He doesn't relax easily. Yet he can joke about it.

One time Cary got so put out with himself that the day before an exhibition match Walter Stewart, sports editor of the Memphis *Commercial Appeal*, found him practicing short pitches and chip shots with a fast, jerky swing.

"What's the idea?" Stewart asked.

"I'm practicing these shots just like I'll be playing them tomorrow," Middlecoff said.

When George S. May raised first prize for the Tam O'Shanter World Championship to $50,000 cash and $50,000 in guaranteed exhibitions, Cary confessed: "I'm afraid Mr. May has reached my choking price. I'd hate to come to the seventeenth hole needing a couple of pars to win that kind of money."

Covering a golf tournament, I've found that some of the best lines come from the caddies. At the Masters tournament at Augusta one year, Middlecoff asked the boy assigned to him what his name was.

"Po'," the boy answered.

"What?" Cary asked.

"Poe. P-o-e."

"Are you by any chance related to the famous Edgar Allan Poe?" Middlecoff cracked.

"I is Edgar Allan Poe," he said, solemn and big-eyed, looking Middlecoff straight in the face.

At the Masters in 1937 I happened to be following Byron Nelson, then a relative unknown, in the rainy Sunday afternoon final round when Ralph Guldahl had finished with a 285 and appeared a certain winner. The 12th hole was a par three and the 13th a par five. Guldahl had played them in 5-6. Nelson scored 2-3 and came in with a 283 for first money.

I asked Byron's caddy, a boy named James Abney, at what stage of the match he thought Nelson was going to win.

"When we bucked dat trey on No. 13, I knowed we was in," he summarized.

I thought Nelson was the finest wooden-club and long iron player I ever saw, and that MacDonald Smith had the best grooved swing. Smith moved to Nashville in the early 1930's, forming a partnership with N. C. Lyon in manufacturing hickory-shaft golf clubs.

To this day it's a mystery how an incomparable stylist such as Mac Smith competed for twenty-six years and never won a U. S. Open or British Open championship. He did tie with his brother Alex and J. J. McDermott for the U. S. Open back in 1910, when he was only eighteen, but Alex won the playoff. Twenty years later, Mac finished two strokes back of Bob Jones in the Open at Interlachen. In between he won many other tournaments, at one stretch averaging 69 strokes for 14 consecutive tournament rounds.

I used to watch Smith practice iron shots by the hour, with that smooth, flawless, never-hurried pace to his backswing, picking the ball neatly off the grass without ever leaving a divot. He had the type of follow-through that many golfers attain only when posing for pictures. He was born to the game; his father was in charge of the Carnoustie links in Scotland, and each of his four older brothers became a professional.

Many people thought Mac Smith was grouchy. The truth was that he was quite deaf and terribly timid. I was not surprised to find his tender inside self when I came to know him, for I had been predisposed to like him by my fondness for another Scot who was gruff and blunt but always true and loyal. This was, and is, George Livingstone, from North Berwick near Edinburgh, who got the job as professional at Nashville's Belle Meade club in 1912 on Grantland Rice's recommendation. George devoted himself single-mindedly to that job for thirty-five years. In retirement he retains an undimmed outlook on life and remains a most trustworthy analyst of golf and of men—whether they be golfers or not.

George would hand a person a cane or an umbrella and watch how casually he held it. Then suddenly he would replace it with a golf club and instantly see the person not only tighten his grip but tighten up all over.

"Golf would be an easy game," Livingstone would say, "if there were no tension. Don't you see? But there's more tension in it than any sport. In other games you're on the move. Motion is the greatest antidote for tension and there is little motion in golf. A man has to condition himself mentally."

The day Livingstone put on bi-focal glasses for the first

time he went out and shot a 68. Maybe his deceiving humor and love of a prank kept him relaxed. One day a club member claimed to be able to hit a golf ball blindfolded. A bet was made. At the last instant George substituted an egg for the ball.

Golf has been described as a sort of psychological mustard plaster; it makes you feel so bad you forget your other troubles. I suppose that can be applied to the pros and duffers alike. But as a sportswriter I find that golf with its first-tee talk, on-the-course conversation and locker-room banter produces some of the most usable extemporaneous quotes and cracks in our business.

Doug Ford, winning the 1957 Masters with a hot last-round 66, labeled himself a scrambler and coined his own title, "King of the Groundhogs."

When Jimmy Demaret appeared one day in one of his loudest ensembles of burnt orange, bright blue and emerald green, Jackie Burke said: "You look like a peacock backing into a sunset."

Demaret, a bit hurt when his protege Burke began to take golf seriously and get to bed early each night during a tournament, christened him Old Curfew Legs: "All his joints close at ten o'clock."

I was playing with Bob Hope in Nashville one time when he whispered that his partner's swing "looked like Kate Smith trying to throw away an old boomerang."

In Tommy Bolt's temperamental days, he was apt to throw his putter after any miss. When he did it in the Bing Crosby tournament, a spectator remarked: "Bolt's putter has more air time than Lindbergh."

The gallery favorite in the 1955 Masters tournament was amateur Billy Joe Patton, who almost won it. He called the rough "Billy Joe country." As he lined up a tough lie in the rough, he noticed the marshals trying to keep the crowd back with ropes. "Go easy on those folks," Patton cautioned

136

the marshals. "They have just as much right to be in the rough as I have."

Another top amateur is Ed Crowley, the "tiger" of the Los Angeles Sheraton Town House, of which he is manager. Both Crowley and his close friend Phil Harris are low handicap players, but when Harris crouches into his putting stance, Ed says he looks as if he's "trying to re-route a varicose vein."

"The worst possible fate to befall a golfer," Harris warns one and all, "is to shoot a 94 and then find out you're in a dry county."

Golf has no strict training rules, as Walter Hagen so often demonstrated. There was another name professional of the Hagen era who became a renowned teacher of the game despite his inveterate swigging. Not long ago young Lew Worsham was playing a round with him, and after each hole this gentleman would gulp a slug of gin, then quickly wash out his mouth with water.

"Why don't you swallow the water instead of spitting it out all the time?" Worsham asked.

"Swallow that water!" the gin hound gasped, horrified. "Hell, man, fish have bathed in it!"

One of the East's best amateurs of the 1920's had the reputation for being able to whip every opponent "except Bobby Jones and John Barleycorn." This fellow is reported to have started out one afternoon at Pine Valley, one of the most difficult courses in the world, with a 3-3-1-3 against a par of 4-4-3-4. The fourth green was near the clubhouse. He went in to get a stiffener and didn't get back on the course for three days.

In September, 1955, the first USGA Senior tournament was held over the Belle Meade course in Nashville. For men fifty-five years of age and over, it is an event marked by its leisurely pace, on and off the course, though the gentlemen combined serenity with a fascinating vigor. The winner, shooting par golf, was Woody Platt of Bethlehem, Pennsylvania. "It takes some people thirty years to find out what causes a hangover," Platt told me. "It's the whisky you drink—after you're drunk."

Platt has a reverential respect for golf. Always he plays in a dress shirt with cuff links, a bow tie, dark blue or gray pants and black shoes. "I would feel I were rude, playing in anything less," he said. "Golf should be treated as a great lady is treated."

I think Chick Evans, another senior, who won the U. S. Amateur and Open in 1916 and still shoots in the low 70's, has the most intense devotion to golf of any man I know. "When my number comes up I hope it's quick, and with a No. 5 iron in my hands," he once said.

Among the golf champions I've followed, Sam Snead unquestionably qualifies as the finest all-round athlete. He would have been outstanding in football, or almost any sport. For one thing, Snead is double-jointed. He can stand on one foot and touch a light globe above his head with the other foot, and he can bend his hand almost flat back against his forearm. Some day I would like to read an intimate, detailed story of Snead's life. I didn't know Sam could play a trumpet, but Red Nichols told me he once inveigled him to sitting in with his "Five Pennies" band for a couple of numbers. Sam is a good dancer and has a pet theory that music wafting over the fairways would help his golf game.

The happiest I ever saw Snead was after he beat Ben Hogan in the playoff for the Masters championship in 1955. After any round, sportswriters like to talk to Sam, though his language often is too picturesque for newspaper use. This day his first comment could be scrubbed up a bit and get by: "The sun don't shine on the same dog's tail every day."

He was asked if Hogan talked to him any during the

round. "Only," Snead cracked, "when he said, 'You're away, Sam.'"

But the main thing was that Sam had come up with a new name for Ben, referring to him only as "The Hawk." Later, writer Herbert Warren Wind expounded on the aptness of this for Hogan: "The grin becomes ironic, and his cold gray-blue eyes widen until they seem to be a full inch in height, and when you look at this man, so furious with himself, he is . . . 'The Hawk.'"

Hogan, only 135 pounds, could hit the ball off the tee as far as most of the big men. He had superlative self-control. It's instinctive in other sports to use maximum speed and power. In golf these instincts must be controlled. That's why Ben could generate such power.

What still puzzles me about Hogan, whom many rate the finest competitive golfer of his day, is how he could practice so long and arduously without losing his zest for the game. It was nothing for him to put in eight-hour stints striving to perfect one little phase of his play. That's where he had the bulge on his brethren of the links. To him, "golf is a game of misses; the golfer who makes the fewest bad shots wins."

Hogan used to have what Ed Miles of the Atlanta *Journal* called a "porcelain" personality. One fellow pro described his smile as a "cross between friendliness and warning that he's fixing to bite you." He mellowed after his miraculous recovery from the auto-bus collision that almost took his life, yet his manner still doesn't court familiarity. He is businesslike—so businesslike, in fact, that he sold the "secret" of his swing to a magazine for a fat fee and cashed in later with the sale of a series of lessons to its sister publication. For the same type of stuff, I doubt if any other professional could have obtained a tenth of the amount of money Ben received.

Yet even Hogan bares some sentiment, particularly for

the Augusta National course, the site of the Masters, saying "it is one of the few courses that can give me real pleasure in playing the day after the tournament ends."

In the good times and life of a sportswriter the Masters tournament gets a top spot. This is the most pleasant spectator event in sports, the best course in the world for seeing golf. It has become one of the game's shrines, and I'm sure that when the vision of such a course and such a tournament first entered the minds of Cliff Roberts, a New York investment banker, and Bob Jones in 1931, neither dreamed it could achieve such an exalted state in so little time. Nature gets credit for a wonderful assist; it would take at least a hundred years to reproduce this paradise in the pine country, built on acreage rich in dogwood and camellias comprising the first nursery in the South.

Does atmosphere—earth and fragrant greenery and trees in bloom and big sky and fresh air—infuse extra "feel" into a writer? Could be. At least it seems to me that general sports columnists who cover only one or two golf tournaments a year, the Masters and/or the National Open, pump a little extra verve into their writings then. And some of the old regulars on the golf beat were tunefully lyrical. England's eminent Bernard Darwin is universally admired for his polyphonic prose, such as this delicate word-portrait of one of the great Scot professionals of the 1880's, Douglas Rolland, who must have been a bit of a rounder:

"Alas! . . . in combined length and accuracy he was the finest driver that ever hit a gutty ball. A magnificent figure of a man, strikingly handsome, with a glorious swing and an innocent happiness in his own powers. 'Awa' she sails wi' dash and spray,' he would explain as the ball sped away. By comparison with his driving, his shorter iron shots and putting were almost crude, a merciful provision of nature that prevented him from being invincible. All agree on his lovableness as a man. He seems to have been one of those to whom the hackneyed phrase was really applicable, that he was no one's enemy but his own. The two traditional pitfalls in the path of mankind were something too much for him. He was by all accounts the most incorrigibly casual and delightful person, doubtless a bad example but a tremendous golfer."

Oscar Bane Keeler was to American golf what Darwin was to the British game, a classicist. He never wrote an obscure sentence or a vapid paragraph. This courtly gentleman, Bob Jones' "Boswell," also was engagingly whimsical—and absolutely unpredictable. Without warning, he would bolt into sonorous recital of some robust epic poem; if introduced to a young lady, he might burst into a love sonnet, then bend gallantly, kiss her hand and say, "I love you madly. Shall we flee together?" But before she could be really alarmed, O. B. would have stood back, sung her a chorus from Gilbert and Sullivan, and limped away on his stiff knee.

I visited him often at the Atlanta *Journal,* eager to see what he was up to next. He was a true artist at his own very special trick of blowing his breath on and polishing with his handkerchief an imaginary glass partition separating the *Journal* sports department from the news room, perplexing no end those strangers who had just joined the staff.

Keeler was always hospitable and polite to callers, but he resented bitterly the telephone, feeling that it intruded into his privacy. One Saturday when the sports staff was tense and hurried putting an edition together, the phone rang and a voice asked: "Hey, settle a bet for us. What was the name of the player who made the touchdown for Columbia that time to beat Stanford?"

"I have no earthly idea," Keeler snapped. "Now you answer a question for me: What was the date of the landing of the ark on Mount Ararat?"

141

O. B. brooded over insulting the caller and regained happiness only when the person complained by letter to the management, giving Keeler the chance to apologize—and add another devoted friend.

I had the privilege of speaking for the newspapermen at a testimonial dinner commemorating Keeler's fortieth year as a newspaperman. He had a talent for writing which was exceeded solely by his zest for living, and with his wit he was a constant source of amusement as well as amazement. His last conscious utterance before he died, in 1950, was a quip. When the interne came in to take a blood sample, O. B., though weak and hopelessly ill, said: "I know who you are. You're Dracula."

People in other countries may not understand American baseball, football, basketball, etc., as reported on the sports pages, but golf is internationally popular. It remained for the Ottawa *Journal*, in Canada, to nail down, only recently, the mysterious origin of the golf term, "take a mulligan." Dave Mulligan, a hotelman in Ottawa, was a constant golfer and he instituted the practice, for himself and his friends, of taking a second shot at the beginning of a round to substitute for a poor first shot.

A sportswriter never knows what to expect on the golf course. My most jarring experience was seeing Art Guepe, the Vanderbilt football coach, swing and then disappear over a 12-foot bluff at Belle Meade, cracking ribs and sustaining internal bruises, and perhaps avoiding a broken neck only by turning a half-flip and landing on his lower back. The next time Guepe played, many weeks later, he wore shoulder-pads and a helmet.

I was playing in a foursome with Billy Graham on Labor Day, 1955, just before he opened a month-long series of sermons in Nashville. Billy swings cross-handed, but at the spot on the course where the biggest gallery had congregated, he holed out 110 yards off the green. Many of those witnesses attended his services that night.

142

John Price Jones, a star of the Broadway musical comedy *Good News* in the 1920's, once showed up on the first tee in Nashville with two caddies. He explained: "I usually have to send one back for laughing."

Unlike most other sports, golf rarely has need for an umpire or a referee. Thus the sportswriter incurs no temptation to find fault in some official. Usually the club professional can settle any question that arises on the golf course. One day at the Richland Club in Nashville a beginner who was getting two strokes a hole from his opponent surprisingly made a 2 on a par-3 hole.

"How should that be marked on the card?" Pro Charlie Danner was asked.

"Just give him a shadow," Danner said.

It was through golf that the most people came to know Babe Didrikson, greatest woman athlete of all time. I recall her first visit to Nashville in 1933, when she basked in Olympic track glory. I thought that if she had concentrated on tennis, instead of golf, with her natural ability and her stamina she would have mastered tennis to a degree no woman ever would have equaled. But Babe chose golf because she liked golf and because golf offered an ease and grace and sociability and enjoyment no other sport could match—for later life.

Which is one of the many cruel ironies in her dying at the age of forty-one.

Bluegrass Is Greener This
Side Of The Fence

In sports' broad field of operations, horse racing spreads the widest crazy-quilt. Its heterogeneous population embraces the breeders, the owners, the trainers, the stable hands, the jockeys, the track operators, the bettors, the pari-mutuel personnel, the bookmakers, the writers and additional assorted gentry and commoners.

The mere fact that the central character—the horse—cannot talk, is no impediment whatever. Rather, this fundamental characteristic stirs the most fanciful hopes and permits limitless post-mortems, for no opinion as to the health, mood or aspiration of a four-legged creature can be totally disproved. With the horse unable to explain why he won or lost, or possibly why he didn't even get to the races, any man has a right to his own conjecture.

But there's a lot more to racing than the race itself. The most pleasant late-April experiences I've had in sports were visits to the horse country in and around Lexington, particularly to the world's foremost Thoroughbred nursery,

144

Claiborne Farm at Paris, Kentucky, presided over so graciously by A. B. (Bull) Hancock and the lady he persuaded to leave Nashville and be his wife, the former Miss Waddell Walker.

At Claiborne I awaken to birds singing, a breeze in the trees and that full-blown fragrance of spring in the Bluegrass blended with the aroma of country ham a-cooking. After breakfast there's a leisurely drive through lush pastures, and against the horizon the memorable silhouette of yearlings clattering uphill, their heels spewing cloddy divots. Then the tranquil scene of more than a hundred colts and fillies at their mothers' sides. Somehow, they never get mixed up; a mare could be taken away for a month and on her return to the field instantly would reunite with her very own foal.

In any phase of horse racing, I never know when I'm going to chance upon column material. On the last visit to Claiborne Stud, it was aces back to back.

First, the spirited stallion Nasrullah, valued at $2,000,000, snortingly paraded his jealousy in a matinee idol performance, kicking the gate to his enclosure and exhibiting further haughty disapproval that visitors would deign to look at and admire his less celebrated equine neighbor, Hill Prince.

Next, in the very antiseptic hospital ward at Claiborne, the stallion Tulyar, imported from Ireland at a cost of $682,000, stood—not lay—desperately ill. When sick, horses stay on their feet; they fear that if they lie down, they won't get up. Tulyar's illness, diagnosed as an intestinal ailment, had been a mass of contradictions. He was insured by Lloyd's of London for $750,000 before his flight from Dublin, and here he was, nibbling on the hand of the veterinarian, Dr. Floyd Sager, who had accompanied him in the plane flying across the Atlantic. In fact, he was almost resting his head on Dr. Sager's shoulder, like a feverish baby. And the horse had been such a national hero in Ireland that

145

each day's mail brought to the Hancocks messages of sympathy and cheer, some enclosing prayers and relics.

Then, a few steps from Tulyar's stall, there was the appealing close-up look at a still-damp foal, barely an hour old, trying to stand on his wobbly legs. Each new arrival is treated as an ultimate Kentucky Derby winner. That's the fascination of the breeding industry. "The true thrill," said Bull Hancock, "comes in choosing the sire and dam, watching the colt develop, then seeing your faith in those bloodlines justified."

Justification must come at the race track. If at Lexington, it's quiet, tasteful Keeneland, which looks like an English print of by-gone days. After lunch in the clubhouse, the late John McNulty said he felt like saying: "Now you folks run along outside on the porch and see the races; I'll stay here and help Mrs. Keene with the dishes." Here racing is a sport before it is a business; there isn't even a public address system blaring the progress of each race. Keeneland seems mellow with the fullness of time, recapturing the ease and informality that marked racing a century ago.

There was a homey touch in this notice posted in the press box by Keeneland's information director, J. B. Faulconer, at the 1957 spring meeting: "The six of hearts is missing from the deck. If it is in your pocket it will be appreciated if you would advise immediately to keep the deck straight."

At Keeneland is the only room named for a sportswriter, the late George Krehbiel, long-time turf editor of the Detroit *News*, a ruddy, free-style fun lover. It's the men's room on the roof near the press box, the door of which is adorned with this metal plaque: "KREHBIEL ROOM. There never was a great man that did not, sooner or later, receive the reverence of his fellow man."

Anyone wanting to enter had to come to George to get the key.

146

Another affectionate reminder of the lighthearted life is the press box elevator at Churchill Downs in Louisville, named "Buck Weaver" for the deceased racing writer of the Louisville *Times* who used to huff and puff and cuss climbing the old stairway. But right there any similarity between cozy Keeneland and bustling Churchill Downs at Derby-time ends. At Keeneland horsehair gets on your coat; on Derby Day at Louisville you might hear a visitor in the milling mob shout, excitedly: "Look! A horse!" Many Derby-goers never see a race.

The Kentucky Derby is a one-day madhouse, with more circus atmosphere and carnival spirit than any show in sports. But for most sportswriters Derby Week begins on Tuesday, and I find that if I don't pace myself for the distance run, I'll be in foul shape by Saturday afternoon, for in our business this is the most strenuous five-day stretch of the year.

For one thing, it's the only time a sportswriter will get out of bed at five or six o'clock for three or four mornings and visit the barns, watch the workouts and talk to the trainers. What he hears and sees may be for immediate use, or he may discover some significant facts to draw upon later. On that same day, near midnight, he's quite likely to be in the Kentucky Hotel suite of Dick Andrade, of Dallas, an oil man and race follower who has a flair for what's festive and who is a perennial Derby host to his newspaper and racing friends.

It's nothing for Andrade to have a Dixieland band flown in from New Orleans and food flown in from New York. And one year when I knocked on his door I was greeted by a trained pony who bowed and stuck out his right front hoof. When this happened to some worse-for-wear late, late callers, many fled without bothering to look back.

Andrade refused to have any part in a stunt to dress up

147

some extremely tall but skinny stranger in complete jockey attire, wearing the colors and number of some lesser-known Derby entry, and let him walk through the crowded lobby of the Brown Hotel on Derby morning, into a cab and out to the track. What puzzled stares and shocking comment that would cause!

Not long ago I asked Ben Jones, the trainer of horses that usually win over $1,000,000 a year for Calumet Farm, how he happened to join this stable in 1938 after winning the Derby with the long shot Lawrin, owned by H. M. Woolf of Kansas City. "Dick Andrade was responsible," he said. "He sold Warren Wright on the idea of getting me. It happened in the summer of 1938 in Chicago. Dick really built me up to Mr. Wright, and he made an offer I couldn't refuse."

Andrade is happiest on pre-Derby nights if he has unearthed some incredible old crony from Texas who has mixed oil and racing and can be persuaded to reminisce. At the 1957 Derby it was T. P. Morgan, of Houston and New York, who admitted to this eventful incident in his life:

"When I was just a young feller in Texas, wearing possum-bellied overalls, one day this stranger came up and wanted to sell a piece of machinery for $2,700. He said it had cost $6,000. I asked what you did with the thing and how it worked. He said that wasn't important, that the main thing was that it was a real bargain. I bought it. It turned out to be an oil drill and I made $468,000 with it."

Before his death in October, 1952, Joe Palmer of the New York *Herald Tribune* was a welcomed and delightful member of any Derby Week group. A native of Lexington and an English instructor first at the University of Kentucky and later at the University of Michigan, he unquestionably was the most scholarly, the ablest and the wittiest racing writer.

148

Palmer had three cardinal cautions: (1) Never bet any horse with a shorter price than 7 to 5; (2) Never trust a man named "Doc" or "Whitey"; (3) Never carry a bundle by a string.

A skilled craftsman with a deep respect for the language and the written word, Palmer also was a spinner of stories. One of his favorites concerned the Kentucky Thoroughbred breeder who had as his guest a titled Englishman. Instead of taking His Lordship on a tour of the barns, the host sat him down on the veranda and had the broodmares and yearlings paraded on halter. White-coated servitors brought out a tray with frosted mint juleps in silver mugs. The host felt highly pleased.

"Can you imagine a finer combination, Your Lordship, than Thoroughbred horses and mint juleps?" he asked.

"You could be quite right," the Englishman said, "but in our country we might say a word for cricket at Lord's and high tea."

One of the colored grooms overheard the remark and said to his partner: "Didn't them gentlemen ever hear of women and watermelon?"

While Joe Palmer was a free indulger in mirth, to him racing was an assignment to be pursued earnestly. The sportswriter who goes on his beat only for big stakes races, such as the Derby, naturally doesn't plow the row as deep. He's hardly to be regarded as an expert, but his newspaper audience expects him to settle on a choice as to the probable winner. And while they would rather he'd be lucky than smart, they feel they're getting more than a simple guess.

Prior to a big race, I rely more on what I hear than on what I see. I try to find the winner by eliminating other horses from consideration. Sometimes this is possible when a jockey can't or won't conceal his low opinion of his horse.

149

Other times a realistic owner will confide certain unfavorable circumstances. A sportswriter comes to know the nature and character of trainers, and how to evaluate their statements.

Before the 1957 Kentucky Derby, Jimmy Jones, training Iron Liege, ultimately 8-to-1 in the betting, volunteered the information, "I think we've found what's wrong with the horse." From Jones, such a statement was worth phoning to the paper, and it looked mighty good in print that afternoon after Iron Liege won.

Notable special assignment writers covering the Derby do not concern themselves with tips or hunches, but their press box comment often is interesting. Such as this, by William Faulkner: "Actually, a jackass has more sense than a Thoroughbred. When he's tired, he quits working. When he can't go on, when the odds are against him, he decides not to do anything. But a Thoroughbred responds to the most disheartening situation. He'll kill himself to try to achieve what's asked of him. So a Thoroughbred must possess a heart as we know it—or conceive of it or think of it."

I think the start of a big horse race is the most pressureful moment in sports. No type of competition, in its first 25 or 30 seconds, requires such intensified alertness and hair-trigger action.

In the starting gate, the jockey in the saddle not only must be rabbit-eared himself for the sound of the buzzer, but he must have his horse head-up and high-tailin'. Once away, in that furious cavalry charge down the lane of howling humans, the little man in the bright silks must make an instant decision: Whether to cut left, bear right, shoot through a hole—a lightning move to gain the best possible position and not get lost in the curving shuffle at the first turn.

I doubt if there is a more electric instant in sports than

150

the start of a Kentucky Derby. Or a more demanding one on the key participants, the jockeys.

The pitcher opening a World Series doesn't have to throw a strike, nor does the hitter have to swing. The football player kicking off is surrounded by encouraging teammates. What if the basketball center is out-jumped on the first tossup? And the sprinter getting set to explode at the start of the 100-yard dash doesn't have to get his horse ready too.

Only comparable situation, for starting pressure, is in golf. Beginning the final round of a big tournament, with a huge gallery watching, suppose a nervous golfer whiffed, missed the ball completely on that first swing?

Sometimes I think that's what some golfer should do, just for the heck of it.

When sportswriters get around to discussing the top athletes of the past 25 or 30 years, I'm amazed how often there's complete omission of jockeys, particularly a rider like Eddie Arcaro. At forty-one, he had won five Derbies, six Preaknesses and six Belmonts.

For reflexes and rhythm, for competitive fire and judgment and balance, and for sports courage, here's one of the most underrated athletes of modern times, one of the true greats, a little man who has risked life and limb hundreds and hundreds of times.

Arcaro has impressed me with two other qualities. This tough little man is one of the most gracious losers I've ever seen; from him, never an alibi.

And he is one of the most intelligent conversationalists in sports, an effortless, meaningful quotesman—and attuned to humor.

When Eddie dismounted in the winner's circle after riding Whirlaway to victory in the 1941 Preakness, he said: "Wipe the jam off my face, I've been on a picnic." Pressed for details of how Whirlaway ran, he cracked: "Well, sorta like driving a Cadillac."

Explaining recently why he no longer bets on horses, because it interferes with his judgment of a race, Arcaro said: "I just make mental bets now. All I'm losing is my mind."

Asked why he, past forty and a millionaire, didn't retire, Arcaro answered: "Because I like being a celebrity. I'm being honest. If some guy who's in the limelight tells you he doesn't like being up there on top, you'd better look at his head. When I retire, I know that I'll be just another little man."

A key man in racing most appreciated by the sports-writers is the chart caller. He calls the name of each horse at regular stages of the race, his exact position and by how many lengths he's ahead of the next horse.

It's an exact science. There's no room for error. If there's a discrepancy in the order the horses are called, the movies will show the mistake.

Numbers on the horses mean nothing to the chart caller. It's all in the colors. He knows all the registered racing colors and he refreshes his memory by murmuring them over and over as the horses parade to the post.

The chart caller stands at the end of the press box, watching through his binoculars, talking quick and clear to a *Racing Form* associate who takes down everything he says in personalized shorthand. It's a remarkable coordination of eye, voice, ear and hand. The chart caller is nearest to accuracy as a human being can be.

Within three minutes after a race is over, the mimeographed chart is ready for distribution throughout the press box. It's official.

I'll never forget the 1957 Kentucky Derby when Iron Liege and Gallant Man pounded across the finish line a nose apart. In the top deck of the Churchill Downs press box, a few writers thought jockey Willie Shoemaker on Gallant Man had stood up in the saddle short of the wire. Could he possibly have mistaken the finish line? The point was being argued hotly when the official chart arrived from the *Racing Form* caller, Don Fair. It said, "Gallant Man . . . was going stoutly when his rider misjudged the finish and he could not overtake Iron Liege when back on stride." That was it—final, irrevocable, official—even before Shoemaker confirmed it to the stewards.

The next day there were quips that Shoemaker had taken a plane for Los Angeles and had pulled up short at Albuquerque, and that a marker would be erected a few yards ahead of the finish line at Churchill Downs, with the inscription: "Willie Shoemaker Slept Here." Two days later Bill Corum, president of Churchill Downs, with other Thoroughbred Racing Associations directors was attending a meeting of the TRA-Grantland Rice Scholarship committee at Vanderbilt University. "We at Churchill Downs are not completely without fault on this," Corum said. "Maybe it is a bit confusing to a rider on Derby Day when there's such a crowd lining the rail. We are going to hang a red disk at the finish line before next year."

It was a typical Corum move, not angrily trying to defend the track, not lambasting the jockey, but facing things fairly and happily and constructively, hoping and trying to better a situation.

Racing is more ably administered, I think, than any sport. That's because it is more nearly a business, conscious of its practical and vital aspect, legal betting. Racing has no fan clubs like the Los Angeles Rams in football or the Milwaukee Braves in baseball. It has no alumni, no faculty, no students, no campus loyalty, no cheering section, no pep rallies. Try to picture some enthusiasts busting into the line at the $2 window and yelling: "All right, men! Let's give a big, loud

'Varsity' for old Aqueduct!" It's no accident that most tracks have real pros as their public and press relations directors. I cannot imagine any project of any kind failing to attract national attention if its promotion and publicity were in the hands of Brownie Leach, Churchill Downs; Everett Clay, Hialeah; Horace Wade, Gulfstream; Bob Kelley, Greater New York; Al Wesson, Hollywood Park; Charlie Johnson, Pimlico, and Gar Moore, Fairgrounds in New Orleans. Most of these were newspapermen at one time. Leach also was schooled under the premier showman who made the Kentucky Derby what it is, Col. Matt Winn.

Clay can think up so many tie-ins with Hialeah's flamingo pink motif that he has been accused of developing his own personal shade of blush when embarrassed during January or February.

The imaginative Wade, who devises multiple gimmicks in his staging of the Florida Derby, admits to being influenced by some of the old-time operators he knew, such as one Martin Nathanson, who at Charleston, South Carolina, in 1910 was trying desperately to capture some customers for his track. A circus arrived in town, and suddenly the thought struck Nathanson that a camel race would stir interest. The circus boss agreed readily.

Five camels were entered and 15,000 Carolinians packed the small track. The bookmakers were swarmed with business. They had no form on the camels, of course, so they called it 4 to 1 on each of the five.

Shortly before the race, however, the bookies noticed the Arab drivers and other handlers of the camels all were betting on a thing called Ben Ali. When the odds went to 7 to 5 on this hot humpback, the bookies closed up shop.

Naturally, they were suspicious. And the track officials were likewise. When the race started, the action of the drivers was studied intently.

From the very start, Ben Ali humped along faster than

154

the other camels. He led for the whole four miles, while his driver placidly gave him his head. The other riders practically de-hided their hapless fleabags and couldn't catch up.

The bookies paid off sullenly to the Arabs. And that night they learned the secret.

After some persuasion, one of the Arabs declared:

". . . There could be no other result. Ben Ali is what we call the bell camel. All their lives, other camels are taught to follow a bell camel.

"You couldn't have driven those other camels past Ben Ali with a bull whip!"

Tracks in Florida and California are becoming so luxuriant that it's almost a downright pleasure to lose in such sumptuous surroundings. I remember accompanying George Davis, sports editor of the Los Angeles *Herald & Express*, to the opening ceremonies of glossy Hollywood Park when it was rebuilt in 1950 following a fire. George kept looking for a "Don't" window in the betting shed, confident that a race track would offer any facility Las Vegas had.

It was at Santa Anita that I heard Braven Dyer say that he went back three generations in horse racing. "I'm losing now on the grandchildren of horses I lost on years ago," he explained.

My top betting thrill happened in New Orleans during the depression, 1931, when I was heading to the Rose Bowl with the Tulane football squad. At the Fairgrounds track, Bill Keefe of the *Times-Picayune* was trying to get back into the good graces of an undersize little man named Harvey, who was a sort of press box attache and called "Wing" because of a deformed arm. Keefe was fond of him, but always pulling gags on him. This day Bill had brought a cheap watch to the track. With the watch concealed in his hand, he asked Wing what time it was, doubted the accuracy of his reply, asked to see Wing's watch, looked at it, shook it close to his ear, said it was no good and, in a quick switch, threw and smashed the cheap watch against the wall while dropping Wing's watch into his pocket.

Almost apoplectic with rage, Wing unloosed the most novel and picturesque profanity I've ever heard.

"I'm sorry I did it," Keefe said in mock apology. "I'll get Pete Baird to put it back together for you. He used to work for a jeweler."

(Baird was and is an assistant to Keefe on the sports staff, and the *Times-Picayune's* page one paragrapher.)

Wing sneered at Keefe in bitter disgust, saying, "The Good Lord and all his disciples couldn't put that watch back together."

While Baird went through the act of assembling the pieces, Keefe said there was a horse named Hazel Denson in the next race which had a chance, though at the moment 90 to 1 on the odds board. Wing reluctantly split a bet with me. The horse won by ten lengths, almost as miraculous as Wing getting his watch back all together and ticking.

The first dog race I ever saw, at Miami in 1932, I bet on a No. 7 dog because the colors were gold and black, the same as Vanderbilt's. He won and paid $96.80 for $2. I had planned to return to Nashville the next morning, but instead took off for a three-day, all-expense trip to Havana. The price: $57.50.

Since then I have "bought" several kennels of greyhounds with scarcely any return on the investments.

Today the state universities and colleges in Florida use money derived from betting receipts at the horse and dog tracks to defray athletic scholarships. This amounts to more than $200,000 a year. In repayment for this effort, I have suggested, without success, that all horses and dogs be admitted free to football games at these colleges.

156

A friend of mine recently coined the beatitude, "Blessed are the poor, for they do not have to attend steeplechases." He had never seen the Iroquois Steeplechase, an annual mid-May event in Nashville, named for the first American horse to win the English Derby, who is buried near the scene of the race.

Here is perhaps the most truly amateur event in racing, staged in one of the most beautiful natural settings.

Nashville's racing heritage is unsurpassed. Charles B. Parmer in his book, *For Gold and Glory,* designates Nashville as the racing capital of America in the 1830's and 1840's. And Belle Meade was one of the country's great breeding farms.

I keep wondering what it would have been like to have been a sportswriter then, and I regret that I can't borrow a few years from those days. Especially would I like to know the details of how the famed filly, Peytona, was walked from Nashville to New York for that celebrated North-South match race with Fashion on May 13, 1845.

Did she actually walk the 900-1,000 miles? How else would a horse have made the trip?

At the time Nashville had no railroad outlet. Travelers to Washington and other Eastern points went by stagecoach. Any kind of horse-drawn wagon or vehicle wouldn't have suited a racehorse.

Peytona could have gone by boat, but that would have necessitated a roundabout journey to Charleston or another Atlantic port.

She must have walked.

The meeting between Peytona and Fashion at the Union Course on Long Island was the race of the century. Currier and Ives immortalized it in a colored lithograph, considered the finest race scene drawn during that period. The New York *Tribune* reported that 70,000 saw the race, and described it:

"Peytona won the first heat by a length. In the second heat . . . as they thundered down the home stretch, Peytona inched ahead and stayed there across the finish line to end the most gallantly contested, as well as the most beautiful race, ever seen in this country."

And then a few days later Peytona walked back to Nashville.

Until a few years ago you could still see the outlines of Andrew Jackson's old race track, traceable in Clover Bottom alongside the highway that leads from Nashville to his home, "The Hermitage." In the early 1800's, Jackson's stallion, Truxton, was recognized as the very finest horse in the whole country. Not only did Truxton hold the record of never having been beaten in a two-mile race when he was in his prime, but according to historian Stanley Horn he sired more than 400 colts "who literally overshadowed all other horses on the tracks."

I don't want to leave Andrew Jackson without calling attention to the advice his mother gave him. They were almost her last words to her young son, and he made them the law of his life:

> Andrew, if I should not see you again, I wish you to remember and treasure up some things I have already said to you. In this world you will have to make your own way. To do that, you must have friends. You can make friends by being honest, and you can keep them by being steadfast. You must keep in mind that friends worth having will in the long run expect as much from you as they give to you. To forget an obligation or to be ungrateful for a kindness is a base crime—not merely a fault or a sin, but an actual crime. Men guilty of it sooner or later must suffer the penalty. In personal conduct be always polite but never obsequious. None will respect you more than you respect yourself. Avoid quarrels as long as you can

without yielding to imposition. But sustain your manhood always. Never bring a suit in law for assault and battery or for defamation. The law affords no remedy for such outrages that can satisfy the feelings of a true man. Never wound the feelings of others. Never brook wanton outrage upon your own feelings. If ever you have to vindicate your feelings or defend your honor, do it calmly. If angry at first, wait until your wrath cools before you proceed.

Remember that Andrew was only fourteen at the time, although he had already enlisted in the American Army, been captured and thrown into prison, where he had smallpox. His mother arranged for his release and nursed him back to health. Responding to an urgent appeal, she left him to go to Charleston to nurse some sick neighbors who were confined there on a British hospital ship. She caught yellow fever and died, leaving the boy an orphan.

At fifteen, Andrew was apprenticed to a saddler. Not long after that, his grandfather Jackson died in Ireland and left the boy a legacy of "about three or four hundred pounds sterling." Andy lost the inheritance at horse races.

But his mother had left him a legacy that couldn't be lost, and he became the greatest man who ever lived in my part of the country.

The Wheel Of The Seasons

Most men in their daily existence move in two worlds: (1) home; (2) the office, store or plant, or wherever their work is. A sportswriter moves in these same worlds—plus eight or ten more.

It's as if sports were a huge merry-go-round, moving with the calendar and partitioned into many sections, alive and bustling. Wherever the play is the most seasonal and the appeal the highest, there's where the sportswriter hops aboard—and rides and lives awhile.

I estimate that approximately forty per cent of a sportswriter's year is devoted to the standard fixtures in athletics, those perennial major events between January and December. A newspaperman in California or Iowa or Tennessee won't necessarily cover the same things, but he will commit the same aggregate of time to the regular occurrences of top interest in his area.

In early spring it's baseball. The sportswriter lives the same kind of life and follows practically the same routine as the player or manager, except for wearing a uniform and taking exercise. Then if he heads for Augusta, and the

Masters tournament the first week in April, he's completely enveloped by the one immediate, consuming interest of the participants and the gallery: golf. At that time golf is the sportswriter's job, his only world; he sets up shop amid the pageantry and the people of that world.

It's the same thing if he's covering any of the sports spectacles: Kentucky Derby, Indianapolis Memorial Day Speedway race, All-Star games, championship prizefights, World Series, bowl football classics, etc. Whatever the arena, he's submerged in the peculiar magic and drama and beauty and wonder of what's to be seen and heard in that particular world.

The Indianapolis "500" is in a class by itself as a sports event that combines spectacle with sound. This automobile race has long attracted crowds surpassing the size of those at almost every other contest involving either men or machines. Time and again, some pseudo-psychologist accuses the crowds of being drawn to the Speedway by the morbid hope of witnessing a fatal wreck. The happier and healthier aspects of the race are far more responsible. There is the contest itself, between drivers and mechanics and cars. There is the split-second efficiency of the teams in the pits. There is the testing of advanced engineering ideas. These all appeal to automotive-minded America.

But for me (a mechanical moron) the "500" is thrilling because of its twin appeal to the eyes and ears. The very best is at the very beginning, when the race is only two minutes old and only one-half of one per cent completed. The thirty-three cars have maintained the symmetry of their ranks in a tight column of threes as they follow the official pace car around the track. And here comes that column of cars down the straightaway at a hundred-and-umpty miles per hour, threatening the pace car with calamity if it doesn't get out of the way. Soon the racers will get strung out, and the laps mixed up in your mind and the contest will go on for hours. But right now the whole show is packed into a picture that the eye can take in although the ear can hardly stand it. The column of cars roars by and away, and your heart beats faster because your eyes and ears have seen and heard sport's most dynamic combination of spectacle and sound.

At the opposite extreme is the unfading memory of sitting quietly on a hillside before dawn, as a boy, when the Tennessee State Foxhunters held their hunts near my home town of Wartrace. That was the most unmechanical sport I've ever known. After nature-invoked silence, which tolerated only the conversation of crickets and rain crows, suddenly but melodiously the dogs would bark their own country music. I didn't know then and I don't know now how a foxhunter can identify, instantly and positively, his own hound's voice. But they did, and do—and who can disprove it? It's one of the why-argue-about-it concessions the sport makes. But the point I make is that foxhunters when they're foxhunting, and boxers when they're boxing, and racers when they're racing, live in a world of their own, and sportswriters who take short-term leases there do the same.

I had been on the sports staff of the *Banner* only a short time when the assignment came to cover a three-day West Kentucky trapshoot at Hopkinsville. I had never been near a trapshoot; I would have been more experienced and hopeful had it been crapshoot. I arranged to ride to Hopkinsville with a cartridge salesman, a nice old man, and picked his brain for what I could. But the real break that probably saved my job was in meeting a most accommodating man named Shelby Peace, a Hopkinsville city official, who gave me a quick education in trapshooting and even edited my dispatches. Later Peace became the president of the Kitty League and kept baseball alive in this Class D territory many years beyond its normal span for these times. But during those three days he and I were in the world of the trapshooters and they had the shades drawn.

As I look back over nearly thirty years, during which the basketball point-shaving scandals soiled and sickened sports, I think that if a person wanted to frame a contest, trap-shooting might be the easiest to rig. That, or possibly corn husking.

I've never seen any contest I suspected was fixed—(I missed each sorry chapter of Primo Carnera's buildup to champion)—but the sport I care least about is boxing. Without question it has deteriorated the most since the late 1920's. I've covered many of the big fights of Joe Louis, Max Schmeling, Jim Braddock, Billy Conn, Joe Walcott, Ezzard Charles and Rocky Marciano, and I've experienced mighty few genuine thrills. I find it an unappetizing assignment, but more likely I've been guilty of just not working hard enough at it. I've come to know very few people in the fight crowd, compared to baseball, football, golf, racing, etc., because I've felt it wasn't worth the time expended; boxing has amounted to little or nothing in the South for many years, and until the advent of television, so ideally suited for boxing, there was in our area a minimum of reader interest in anything below the heavyweight division.

The South has produced surprisingly few successful boxers. Young Stribling of Macon, Georgia, finally got a shot at the heavyweight crown against Jack Sharkey but never lived up to expectations. Beau Jack, of Augusta, was lightweight champion. Joe Louis was born in Alabama but left at a very early age for Detroit; Michigan has claim to him. Yet even more astonishing is the fact that not a single world, U. S. or national intercollegiate record in track is held by a Southerner.

Duke University's brilliant Dave Sime, holder of the world's record in the 220-yard dash (20.0) and 220-yard low hurdles (22.2) and one of four tied for the 100-yard dash record (9.3), lives in New Jersey. The majority of the other U. S. record holders are from California. The one time a Southern squad won the national collegiate track championship was in 1933, when Louisiana State, coached by the present Southeastern Conference commissioner, Bernie Moore, had such stars as Slats Hardin, Al Moreau, Jack Torrance and Matt Gordy. Maybe it's just too hot to run fast, and far, in the Deep South.

A marked exception is the Negro woman track athlete in the South. The most rapid championship development I've witnessed in sports was at Tennessee State A & I University in Nashville; in little more than a year, five women athletes qualified for the 1956 U. S. Olympic squad. At Melbourne, Isabelle Daniels, holder of the world's indoor record for the 50-yard dash (5.8), finished fourth in the 100-meter dash. Willie White finished second in the Olympic women's broad jump. The A & I team ran third in the 400-meter relay. These "Tigerbelles" also won the 1956 National AAU indoor and outdoor team championships.

Track seems the most demanding and, unless an athlete can win a place on the Olympic squad, the least rewarding sport. I've always regarded two-mile runners as the most lonesome of men. And the late Bill Alexander used to say: "The only people interested in discus throwers are the sculptors." Then, is there any real future in shot-putting?

This reminds me of a gag at the expense of the late Frank Thomas when he was University of Alabama's athletic director and football coach, and all the coaches used to gather at the annual Southeastern Conference track meet in Birmingham. Though a well-conducted, interesting show, the meet never attracts many spectators. Prior to the Saturday finals the Chamber of Commerce tendered the visiting sports people a luncheon at which we framed Bill Tucker, then a new United Press correspondent from Atlanta and unknown to the guests, to appear as the booking agent for a professional track troupe. Bill made his pitch that he wished to bring his group—a shot-putter, discus thrower, javelin man, broad jumper and two-mile runner—on an exhibition tour of a few Southern college campuses, and that they could appear on successive afternoons at Athens, Georgia, Auburn and Tuscaloosa, Alabama, Oxford and Starkville, Mississippi, for a guarantee of only $750 at each place.

Even before Tucker finished and sat down, the sheer absurdity and financial folly of such a proposal had, quite noticeably, offended the intelligence of the wily Thomas. Thus he was outraged when first Wally Butts of University of Georgia and then Dudy Noble of Mississippi State arose (by prearrangement) and subscribed to the idea, pledging the requested guarantee. When Thomas got his chance to talk, he was so expressive in his denunciation that all stags there enlarged immeasurably their vocabulary of salty phrases.

One trouble with track as a spectator sport is that a track meet suffers from its own excesses as a spectacle. It is spread all over the place and all over the afternoon. There is no single, simple, ever-recurring point of focus such as football's scrimmage line and baseball's batter *versus* pitcher. And that little Latin word *versus* is the biggest word in competitive sport. It means turned toward; it connotes conflict, opposition, attack against defense, a man or team trying to do a thing while another man or team tries to block or stop or somehow prevent that thing. In track the contestants are not *versus* each other; they face the same direction. They are not contestants against each other so much as they are contestants against the clock and the measuring tape. That's why running a great race is a great mental achievement. Quite truly, somebody said of John Landy, after his 3:58 mile, that what Landy had done better than anybody else in the world was to calculate his strength accurately and spend it out precisely so as to exhaust it completely in 5,280 feet exactly.

As a spectacle to be depicted in newspaper stories, I think the Olympic Games now stand alone. That's because of the drastic change television has wrought in the sportswriter's approach to his coverage of the major events in the United States. If they're televised, he can practically forget about any description of the crowd and the color; the viewers can see that for themselves. He must concentrate on what they don't see and hear, or on what they see and hear and still don't understand fully.

When UCLA was penalized for coaching from the sidelines in the 1956 Rose Bowl game against Michigan State, it resulted in one of the most hectic finishes in football history. With the score tied 14 to 14, UCLA was trying to pass from behind the goal line in the last minute of the game, instead of killing time, and lost 17 to 14 on Dave Kaiser's 31-yard field goal with seven seconds remaining. In such a situation, the sportswriter doing the best job was the one who could find out exactly what had happened on the bench to cause the penalty, and the UCLA players' conversation in their huddles on their last sequence of plays. This is when it pays to have a close friend on the coaching staff or among the players.

Only thing better than a friend is two friends. In the third game of the 1952 World Series, Brooklyn beat the Yankees, 5 to 3, scoring two runs in the ninth inning when a pitch by Tom Gorman got past catcher Yogi Berra. Berra was being measured for horns by most of the 66,698 cash patrons and 600 non-paying residents of the press box. This put Brooklyn ahead, two games to one, and might prove to be the decisive play of the Series.

166

In the dressing room after the game there was as much confusion as there had been among the official scorers who first called the play a wild pitch and then a passed ball. Manager Stengel didn't know exactly what happened. Berra and Gorman weren't saying anything. Jim Turner, Yankee pitching coach, who wisely avoids all dressing room interviews, referred newsmen to Stengel.

I was rushing to catch a plane for Chicago, where Vanderbilt and Northwestern were playing football the next day. I asked Tom Meany, then with *Collier's*, if he would approach Turner later, see what he could find out, and file an overnight piece for me.

Turner revealed that when Gorman came back to the Yankee bench after pitching the ninth inning, he sat by him. "Looks like you crossed Yogi up on that pitch?" Turner said. It was only then that it dawned on Gorman that Berra had called for a fast ball—and he had thrown a curve. "Golly, I did," Gorman said.

A catcher's signs haven't changed since you were a kid. It's still one finger for the fast ball, two for the curve and a wiggle of the fingers for a change-up. The only thing which varies is the combination in which the signs are given. A catcher gives three or four or five, but there is an identifying sign which tips off which signal is the McCoy. Berra had gone through the usual complicated digital manipulation, but Gorman read them wrong.

The Yankees went on to win the Series, but at that time, the thing most people wanted to know was exactly what happened on that one pitch.

There are many World Series games, of course, wherein nothing spectacular or extraordinary or controversial happens. That's when I'm doubly grateful for the press headquarters, usually a large dining room at a hotel designated by the home club, where newspapermen and the baseball managers and coaches and scouts assemble after the game for refreshments and food and—until well into the morning— talk.

Casey Stengel almost always is holding court in the press headquarters, whether or not the Yankees are in the World Series. Among all people in all sports, Casey consistently furnishes the most quotable material for sportswriters—if they can follow his strange syntax. For, with all his knowledge of baseball, his master strategy, his manipulation of players, the remarkable Stengel is also a clown. Outside the entertainment field, I've known no one with a keener feel for comedy.

Frank Graham was talking about Yogi Berra's odd build, and Stengel reminded Frank and everybody else that he had an odd build, too.

"When I was playing with Brooklyn," Casey said, "and Wilbert Robinson was managing, I had a little difficulty catching this fly ball for the last out in a game, and as we are going into the clubhouse, Robby growls at me. I ask what's the matter now and he says:

" 'What were you staggering around under that ball for?'

" 'I got it, didn't I?' I say, and he says:

" 'Yes, but you give me heart disease every time you go after a ball.'

"Then he says: 'Oh, well, with a rump and legs like that, you shouldn't even be a ballplayer.'

" 'I shouldn't, hey?' I says. 'What should I be?'

"And he says: 'I was trying to think, but I give up.' "

Some of Stengel's most savory conversation doesn't pertain to sports. I'm one who thinks sports page readers relish such off-beat stuff—if it crackles—no matter if it isn't sport. Any time is laugh time. One of Casey's funniest discourses was on the subject of midgets, recorded by Gerald Holland of *Sports Illustrated* like this:

168

" 'Midgets are smart,' Stengel said, thrusting his thumbs behind his belt, 'smart and slick as eels. You know why?'

"He looked around.

" 'It's because,' he said, 'they're not able to do much with the short fingers.'

"He held out his fists with the fingers tucked in.

" 'You understand?' he asked. 'Not being able to do anything with their fingers, what do they do?'

"He tapped his forehead.

" 'They develop their brain power.'

"His audience listened respectfully.

" 'Short people tend to be smarter all along the line,' said Casey. 'You take bartenders. A short bartender will outperform a tall bartender every time.'

"By way of proving his point, Stengel 'became' a tall bartender, standing on tiptoes and bending over to pour drinks. Seems the constant bending over by the tall bartender develops a back misery and 'he's out of there in a few hours.'

"Then Casey bent his knees and 'became' a short bartender, with the bar hitting him at shoulder level.

"Casey shot his arms straight out and back like pistons.

" 'Whsst! Whsst! Whsst!'

"He looked around, his arms working furiously in demonstration of a short bartender serving drinks.

" 'You get it?' he cried. 'No back strain whatever. He can go all night.' "

Unfortunately, the World Series press room can present a certain hazard. For years there was a Southern sports editor covering the World Series who could resist everything but temptation. He seldom made it past the first game, and there was talk of getting him listed officially among the records in Al Munro Elias' *Little Red Book* under the cate-

169

gory: Most Times Passed Out Under Table. Whenever this happened, some friend always filed a story for the fallen brother, most often obtaining a carbon of what Tommy Holmes had written for the late, lamented Brooklyn *Eagle*, the newspaper least likely to be seen in the errant delegate's home town. It was Holmes, by the way, who after the *Eagle* folded, wrote: "Brooklyn is the only metropolitan city in the United States that has no railroad station, no daily newspaper and no left-fielder."

Bowled Over

From time to time I've heard lots of people say: "If I had plenty of money and didn't have to work, I would just travel from one big sports event to another." I wouldn't guarantee their enthusiasm would last on such a steady diet, but there are any number of people—hundreds of thousands—who habitually attend some of the big events and for awhile get immersed in the sportswriter's natural habitat.

Sports are such an integral part of American life that I know many people who look on Yankee Stadium, for example, as hallowed ground. Even when no game is being played, they can go there, stand and recapture the scene of Babe Ruth at the plate thirty years ago, just as journeyers to the battlefield at Gettysburg can visualize Pickett's charge.

Visitors would hardly leave the Notre Dame campus without seeing the stadium and the Knute Rockne Memorial. At no university is the tradition so linked with football. The most non-athletic sophomore knows about the immortal George Gipp, super-fullback of 1919-20, and the cold December day that he died, in his senior year, as the chapel bells tolled and the student body knelt in the snow to pray. On the day of a big game, the Notre Dame scene is the most electric I've experienced. Each time, I can almost hear the heart-beat of tradition thumping. It affects all opposing teams; some get so zinged-up they transcend themselves, others scare. Even in the press box, few are completely immune to the emotional excitement.

Three of the most thrilling games I've seen were at Notre Dame. In 1931 I saw Southern California score 16 points in the fourth quarter to beat the Irish, 16 to 14, on Johnny Baker's field goal. Notre Dame's 14-13 edging of the pro-loaded Iowa Seahawks in 1943 was a whing-ding. But for sustained action, my all-time throbber was the 1952 score-athon: Notre Dame 27, Oklahoma 21. Seven touchdowns, but never more than seven points difference between the teams . . . the kind of hitting that caused 21 fumbles, 13 in the first half . . . from the first minute to the sixtieth, not one languid instant.

Body contact, youth, tradition and spirit make football the sports spectacle with, I think, the most wallop.

When I got into sportswriting in 1929, the Rose Bowl was the only New Year's Day football game. There was an allure about the Rose Bowl trip which no other postseason attraction has matched. The cross-country trek to California with such teams as Tulane, Alabama and Tennessee was a young sportswriter's dream, with their stopovers at El Paso (always a side trip to Juarez, Mexico), Tucson and the Grand Canyon.

I remember a Tennessee lineman's comment upon his first look at the Grand Canyon: "Boy, that would be a helluva place to lose a cow!"

And the wistful look on the face of Bernie Bierman, Tulane coach who was raised in Minnesota, watching grown

Joe Engel, Chattanooga baseball club owner, gets the happiest mileage out of life of anybody I've known in sports. He's stayed young with a wonderful sense of humor.

Bud Wilkinson—For him the na[me] Galahad would be much more fitti[ng]

Bear Bryant can lift a football squad to the stratosphere. He injects more of his own fire into a squad than any coach I know.

Performers like Charlie Trippi happen so seldom. All-American and All-Pro, he's my choice as the all-time, all-purpose college backfield performer.

This is a Father's Day picture of myself and our four daughters. I sat with Lee and Carolyn, while Kay and Ellen stood behind us.

A favorite of mine is this photograph of Kay, Carolyn, wife Kay, Lee and Ellen on the lawn of our home in Nashville.

Just before we all headed for Sunshine Park, Kay took this snapshot of
Grantland Rice and me at St. Petersburg in March 1952. I don't recall
how we came out after the day's racing, but no one ever "lost" if Granny
was with him.

Eddie Arcaro, a great jockey, holds up five fingers in the Churchill Downs tackroom to signify his unprecedented fifth Derby victory in 1952. I'm peeking behind Arcaro's hand. (*AP photo*)

One year later, it's a serious-sided Eddie as he explains to Keeneland stewards that he wasn't guilty of rough riding. (*AP photo*)

One of my top thrills came when heroes of the Golden Age—Red Grange, Bob Jones and Jack Dempsey—were in Nashville for the dinner that commemorated my twenty-fifth year as Banner sports editor in 1953.

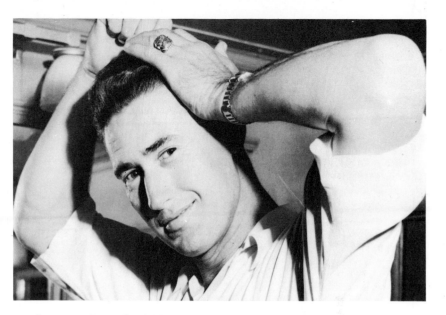

"I can pick up the ball as soon as it leaves the pitcher's hand and follow it up to a point maybe two or three feet in front of the plate." That's what Ted Williams claims—and is there a pitcher alive who refutes this statement?

Phil Harris and Red Sanders, together in Los Angeles, shedding sentimental tears over their boyhood days in Nashville. Remember Red as a Vanderbilt undergraduate a few photographs ago?

Don't ask for the handicaps. But we all had a fair day at the Belle Meade
Country Club in 1954. The foursome was Billy Graham (the preacher who
plays the game cross-handed), Tennessee Governor Frank Clement and
Nashville businessman Russell Brothers.

It was a fitting farewell from football for Otto Graham (*left*) after leading the Cleveland Browns to the pro title in 1956. Coach Paul Brown and Graham made the Browns one of sports most powerful grid machines.

The portrait of Grantland Rice, by Willard Mullin, was the backdrop for the head table at the memorial dinner at Shor's November 1, 1954, as I talk with Tom Meany.

At the first Grantland Rice Memorial Award luncheon in 1955—John (Terry) McGovern, vice-president of The Sportsmanship Brotherhood, was toastmaster; John Kieran and Bruce Barton, speakers.

Bowden Wyatt (*right*), Tennessee's 1938 captain under coach Bob Neyland, came home to command the Volunteers and be named the 1956 Coach of the Year. He couldn't have had a better teacher than General Robert.

Casey Stengel's foremost managerial quality is the way
he delegates authority to his coaches, for example Nash-
villian Jim Turner, who handles the pitchers masterfully.
(*AP photo*)

These Southern Sportswriters who assembled at a *Banner* banquet
in 1957 represented 200 years of sportswriting. Standing: Zipp
Newman, Birmingham *News*; Tom Siler, Knoxville *News-Sentinel*;
Walter Stewart, Memphis *Commercial-Appeal*; and *Banner* publisher
and ex-sportswriter James G. Stahlman. Seated: Fred Digby, New
Orleans *Item* before he became general manager of the Sugar Bowl;
Ed Danforth, longtime Atlanta sportswriter; Russell.

Toots Shor congratulates Willie Hartack, the 1957 Kentucky Derby's winning jockey, as Frank Graham and I look on. Willie made it, you will remember, when Willie Shoemaker, aboard Gallant Man, misjudged the finish pole.

Horse haven is the Claibone Farm at Paris, Kentucky. "Bull" Hancock and Mrs. Hancock check on spirited Nasrullah which is valued at two million dollars.

Two of my fondest friends, Red Smith (*left*) and Bill Corum, are also two of the top writers in this wonderful world of sport.

Louisiana boys seeing and feeling snow for the first time. They wallowed in it.

Something real good went out of football when the special trains gave way to the planes.

The Rose Bowl gave Southern football its biggest lift nationally when those first Alabama teams in 1925 and 1926 beat Washington and tied Stanford. An added tinge of glamor caught the public fancy when Johnny Mack Brown, star 'Bama halfback, made good in the movies. But the best Rose Bowl team I ever saw didn't come out of Dixie. It was the 1931 Southern California squad, coached by Howard Jones, a unit of wonder-working power with six players who made All-America during their careers, including destructive tackle Ernie Smith and superior halfback Ernie Pinckert.

In 1947 the Tournament of Roses began to match Pacific Coast Conference teams against Western Conference teams exclusively. The Big Ten claimed Southern schools were using the money they derived in Rose Bowl receipts to recruit players in Big Ten territory. I doubt if any such charge would ever have been made had not Frank Sinkwich, from Youngstown, Ohio, and later Charlie Trippi from Pennsylvania, developed into such outstanding halfbacks at the University of Georgia. The Big Ten condemned the athletic scholarships established by the Southeastern Conference in 1935, which provided football players tuition, room, board and books. Now, finally, the Big Ten has adopted a similar type of scholarship as the Southwest Conference, the Big Seven, the Atlantic Coast, the Southern and others did years ago. This is solid vindication for the originator of the plan, Dr. John J. Tigert, and one of the keenest satisfactions I've had.

Dr. Tigert, a giant of a man, had been All-Southern fullback at Vanderbilt in 1901-02 and was Tennessee's first Rhodes Scholar. He coached at University of Kentucky, was U. S. Commissioner of Education, then president of the University of Florida. As president of the Southeastern Conference in the early 1930's, Dr. Tigert confided his deep concern over the accepted practice of college football players signing eligibility blanks swearing they were receiving no financial aid of any kind, when it was common knowledge that all the top players were provided sinecures. He evolved the idea of recognizing athletic ability in awarding scholarships, remembering that his own athletic activity had been considered an asset, not a deficiency, when he was competing for a Rhodes Scholarship. With many large universities now netting $250,000 to $500,000 annually from football gate receipts, Dr. Tigert's plan seems not improper —unless the college desires itself to be professional but its players to be amateur.

I think the athletic scholarship is the best plan, but it isn't perfect. The worst feature is that it gives the football coach excessive power over the player. Some coaches abuse it. Some players lose their independence, for they know the coach can cut them off the scholarship. They will submit to inconsiderate treatment, because not to might suddenly bring an end to their college education. Some boys get to feeling that they are working for the coach, instead of playing for the school.

By 1935 the Rose Bowl had serious competition. So many bowls were springing up that Dan Parker (New York *Daily Mirror*) feared "every city might have a bowl game except Flushing, N. Y."

The Sugar at New Orleans, the Orange at Miami and the Cotton at Dallas now equal the Rose at Pasadena in national stature and attention. The Sugar is a monument to the vision, venture and follow-through of one man, Fred Digby, now its general manager, who campaigned for it relent-

174

lessly in his years as sports editor of the New Orleans *Item.* Every year, these games spoon up full measures of holiday enjoyment in the life and good times of a sportswriter.

The big bowls are here to stay. I think their future has been assured by the money-division all conferences have adopted. When one member school plays in a bowl, all others share in the swag. I've found that nothing soothes the criers of football overemphasis as quickly as a few thousand dollars sliding into the college's athletic treasury.

But I predict the format of bowl games will be changed by television. Already the smaller Gator Bowl at Jacksonville, Florida, has gained the biggest TV audience by shifting its game to the Saturday before New Year's Day whenever possible. The Pacific Coast time differential assures the Rose Bowl game an undivided late-afternoon audience. But the Orange, Sugar and Cotton Bowl, in direct competition, are in my opinion the worst buy in television for the sponsor. The instant a commercial comes on, ninety per cent of the viewers will switch to another channel, hoping for live action. In more and more homes, New Year's is a TV holiday with families and guests planning their schedule around the games. I wonder, among the Sugar, Cotton and Orange Bowls, which will be first to shift its game to 10:30 or 11 o'clock in the morning? The game-goers themselves won't mind; they would like to get back home to watch the other bowls on TV.

Let's face it, money is the determining factor in the staging of practically all sports events, pro or amateur. I was a midwife at the birth of the Senior Bowl game, now an annual early January attraction at Mobile, Alabama,—a reluctant midwife, because I wasn't at all sure that the baby could live. Here's how that game originated:

Jimmy Pearre, a Nashville general contractor, came to me

with the idea that college seniors, after they had completed their football eligibility, should have the chance to play in a game and get $400 to $500 out of it.

I told him I thought the colleges would oppose the idea bitterly. It was too professional.

"Why?" Pearre asked. "Many colleges have paid their players as much as $250 apiece when their teams went to a bowl. Then, lots of the players who appear in these post-season all-star games not only get liberal expenses, and watches, and trips for their wives, but they are slipped $100 or $150 under the table. Why not give it to them out in the open?"

I said that for one thing, it would make them ineligible for other sports in the remainder of their senior year. Some played basketball or baseball, or went out for track.

"We won't go after any football players who are outstanding in another sport," Pearre proposed.

I said I still doubted if the coaches would want their players to participate in a game where one man or group of men would stand to profit. It would have to be for some charitable or civic purpose to get the support of the people, the newspapers and all essential agencies, wherever it was played.

Pearre said that was precisely what he had in mind, that he would retain a certified public accountant from the out-set, that he wanted to make it worthwhile for some city, that all he expected, after it was established, was a nominal salary.

But who would coach the teams?

"Professional coaches," he said. "It's a natural for the pros, getting to see all those college seniors on one field, in one game."

Well, this positive-thinking little man quickly sold Coach Steve Owen of the New York Giants and Coach Bo McMillin of the Detroit Lions, then lined up Red Grange to help

176

him put the thing over. Pearre was a bulldog the way he stayed with his pet project. Whenever anybody said no, he just smiled and thanked them and moved on. He got the backing of three Nashville business men, and they selected Jacksonville as the site of the first game on January 7, 1950. Fifty seniors were brought in and divided into North and South squads with Owen and McMillin as opposing coaches. Doak Walker of Southern Methodist was pitted against Charlie Justice of North Carolina as the headline attractions. It was an action-filled game, the South winning, 22 to 13, but only 16,000 turned out and there wasn't enough money to meet expenses. Jacksonville seemed more interested in its Gator Bowl game. At a meeting that night in a room at Ponte Vedra Inn, the decision had to be made to try again the next year—or chuck it. The backers put up more money, and began looking for another city.

Mobile needed an attraction to grace its new Ladd Memorial Stadium. Civic leaders there, headed by J. Finley McRae, president of the Merchants National Bank; Ed Roberts, Frank Leatherbury and others listened to Pearre and his liaison man, Mobile's own affable Pat Moulton, then public relations director of Waterman Steamship Corporation. They took on the game and organized the Mobile Arts and Sports Association, a non-profit corporation, to channel all net earnings into a youth recreational program and other activities wholly devoted to public benefit.

At each Senior Bowl game I marvel at the smooth team play despite so little practice. Boys who have never seen each other before are welded into functioning offensive and defensive units within four or five days. Those seniors arriving late from their New Year's Day bowl games sometimes practice only three days. It helps some, of course, that the players on the winning squad are paid $500 each, the losers $400. Yet the consistently brisk performances, regularly attracting crowds of 30,000, are a source of some

177

embarrassment to the many coaches who would make football such a mysterious and complex operation, understood by a very privileged few.

Steve Owen employed the personal touch and made good use of the needle in his accelerated—and successful—Senior Bowl coaching. More than once, starting the first day's practice, I've heard him shout to an assistant this penetrating distinction: "You take charge of the backs and ends; I'll handle the men."

In 1951, one of Owen's halfbacks was Jack Jones from little Livingston, Alabama, Teachers College, not far from Mobile. Supporters from there formed a loud rooting section behind the South's bench, shouting "We want Jack Jones! We want Jack Jones!" Finally Owen summoned Jones, who dashed to his side peeling off his jacket. "Go up in the stands," Owen said. "Some folks up there want you." He was kidding, of course, shortly thereafter putting Jack into the game.

Humor is standard equipment in football, especially pro football, and Owen ranks with Jack Lavelle and Jimmy Conzelman as its premier practitioners within my time.

Paul Brown of the Cleveland Browns, who now coaches in the Senior Bowl every year, is the best organizer I've seen in football. But to me he isn't the cold, dedicated precisionist who only talks, eats and sleeps football, as so often pictured. Indeed, there are times when Brown all but outlaws football talk. Know what the Cleveland coaching staff does just before the season's practice begins each July? They play ten different Ohio golf courses in ten days and if anyone mentions football, his comment must be (a) mighty funny or (b) mighty helpful.

Among the sports personalities I've had a chance to know, Brown is one of the true standouts—perceptive, intelligent, articulate. Once I asked him to put into the fewest words possible his reasons for the greatness of Otto Graham, for many years pro football's No. 1 quarterback. Brown summarized: "He's the most poised, the most polished, with a knack of sliding, ducking, leaning, twisting a shoulder or turning a hip to escape tacklers, yet never getting out of the passing pocket. He has a phenomenal right wrist; he can throw the ball forty yards with just a flick of his wrist. He has exceptional quarterbacking personality: he's magnetic, generous, takes blame, never second-guesses, never worries." Such informative conciseness makes sportswriters live longer.

Unlimited substitution is permitted in Senior Bowl games. All pro coaches like it, and a lot of the college coaches wish their rules still allowed it. They claim the use of offensive and defensive specialists increases individual proficiency beyond measure, and certainly it should. Yet none of the accomplished experts developed during college football's platoon era, as I recall, has won the title of Football's Greatest Runner—or passer or punter or blocker or tackler. Indicating, I think, that playing both offense and defense never did limit the opportunity for individual excellence or maximum effort. And never will.

I get a special kick out of watching the Senior Bowl players who have been named on All-American teams, for since 1949 I have been writing the annual "Pigskin Preview" for *The Saturday Evening Post* in which I make a guess, in September, as to what eleven players are going to make All-American and which teams will finish as the nation's top twenty. It's more of a distillation of appraisals than a set of predictions, for I analyze reports and opinions from more than 200 key operatives among coaches, sportswriters, scouts, college athletic information directors and players themselves. Obviously it's risky business, and I'm sure no person in the world reads with more interest than I do the consensus All-American selection and the press services' top twenty teams when they appear at the end of the season.

How often does the All-American player prove superior to his opponents or to his own teammates in the bowl games? About as often as not—no more. I couldn't pick 'em much better in January than I do in September.

Press Box View

A sportswriter spends a considerable portion of his life in an elevated workshop called a press box. At most ball parks, stadiums, race tracks, etc., this extended cubicle with the picture window provides a splendid panoramic view of the proceedings below—a view which no newsman covering an event can revel in, however. If he isn't typing a story or column during a game, he's trying to fashion and mentally stitch together some thoughts to put on paper afterward.

Cross my heart and hope to die, the man is working.

As he sweats and possibly bleeds a little, he may try to delude himself: "Sportswriting would be the perfect life—— if I didn't have to write."

He knows, of course, this isn't true. Pleasure rests on contrasts. Champagne every night would lose its sparkle. Fun all the time would cease to be fun. The truest enjoyment comes from amusement and surprises and sudden twists, mixed with work.

A sportswriter in his pursuit of what's significant or entertaining or unusual may tarry before going to the press box, and at times not fruitlessly. Prior to one of Vanderbilt's opening football games I chanced upon the team trainer, Smoky Harper, who expressed deep concern as to the outcome. And why? "Because we haven't had enough live scrimmaging," he said. "Nothing but all that dummy work. But I'll say this: If we ever run up against a team of dummies, we'll stomp hell out of 'em."

If it's baseball the sportswriter is covering, he won't draw many blanks dropping by the batting cage or the bench before the game. One afternoon John Carmichael, of the Chicago *Daily News,* was listening to a rookie questioning a veteran slugger on a purely technical item:

"When you hit, do you keep your left foot forward or is it better to keep both feet even and far apart?"

"Young man," the oldster answered, after considering the question briefly, "when you step up to the plate, never be superstitious."

On the subject of pitching, Satchel Paige talking on the bench before a game might be more revealing: "I got bloopers, loopers and droopers. I got a jumpball, screwball, a wobbly ball, a whipsy-dipsy-doo ball, a hurry-up ball, a nothin' ball and a bat dodger."

I heard Art Fowler, Cincinnati pitcher, once summarize the "junk" assortment thrown by another right-hander, Saul Rogovin of the Phillies: "You could catch him with a pair of pliers."

Sometimes just a few words heard on the field can reveal instantly an athlete's personality. Nashville hired as its 1957 baseball manager Dick Sisler, oldest son of the all-time great, George Sisler, and like his father a first baseman. Dick has an impediment in his speech and I wondered if it would bother him, if he would be sensitive about it, when he started his players into spring training. Before the workout began the first day, Sisler told about stopping in a filling station for gasoline en route to Florida.

"The attendant came up to the car window," Dick said,

"and he stammered, 'H-h-h-how m-m-many g-g-g-gallons?'
This was an awful t-t-ough s-s-pot for me, 'cause I stammer
too, and I thought he would f-f-feel I was mocking him. I
started to d-d-drive off. But I said, 'F-f-fill 'er up,' and he
just looked at me funny and w-went about his business."
Thus Sisler gave early and definite notice that he wasn't at
all sensitive about his stuttering.

John Drebinger, well-known New York *Times* baseball
writer, wears a hearing aid. One spring day at St. Petersburg,
Casey Stengel conspired with Drebinger's fellow writers.
When they all assembled at the Yankees' bench and began
asking questions, Casey kept his mouth working, as if talking, but shut off his voice. Some of the writers began taking
notes furiously, others looked at their watches and rushed
for telephones while Drebinger slapped and shook his hearing aid angrily, and cursed. John is the kind who laughs as
heartily as anybody about such a gag, and at his press box
typewriter is a fair hand at poetry, such as this doggerel
about the little-known managers who recently have come
into major league baseball:

> Nobody heard of Mayo Smith;
> We thought Walter Alston was a myth;
> But now we're really over the barrel—
> Who in the hell is Kerby Farrell?

Roy Stockton, sports editor of the St. Louis *Post-Dispatch*,
weary of and annoyed by the perennial spring exhibition
bromide that "the hitters are ahead of the pitchers," waits
for the first infield error to remove his pipe and say, dryly:
"The grounders are ahead of the fielders."

After Vic Janowicz, former Ohio State All-American halfback, reported to the Pittsburgh Pirates as a catcher, sports
editor Chet Smith of the Pittsburgh *Press* was asked how
Vic was faring. "Well, he can't hit or field or throw much,"
Chet said, "but he's all right carrying the ball."

Later in a game Janowicz was struggling under a high foul, going forward, backward, right and then left, when a loud fan bellowed: "Why don't you signal for a fair catch?"

The press box is the birthplace of many spoken lines which later find their way into print, such as Tom Meany's unforgettable description of unforgettable Rudy York: "Part Indian and part first baseman." It was Meany, watching the Yankees and Dodgers with their 1943 war-time personnel, who quipped: "Neither looked like either."

There are times when writers in the press box compose lead paragraphs purely for the consumption of their typewriter neighbors, then overwhelmed by the responsive laughter decide to try to slip them in their newspapers. The late Harry Williams, eulogizing a Los Angeles pitcher who toiled long and admirably only to lose, got away with this:

"Mr. Arthur Summers Sutherland pitched his initials off yesterday as our Los Angeles nine went down to defeat, 1 to 0."

Occasionally there is shop talk in the press box, comments on how this or that columnist filled his space in recent days. One time Jimmy Cannon of the New York *Post* had quoted some Florida waitresses who said that fishermen as a breed were both abusive and poor tippers. "If Mr. Cannon says he has done research with waitresses, I have no right to dispute him," Red Smith of the *Herald Tribune* said. "But if he talked fishing with 'em, it was the biggest form reversal since Jim Dandy won the Travers."

Smith's wry humor works overtime. In the Churchill Downs press box at Louisville he received a telegram from the editor of Vanderbilt's alumni magazine, requesting permission to reprint one of his recent columns about the Grantland Rice Scholarship established by the Thoroughbred Racing Associations. Smith wired this reply:

"Of course you're welcome to reprint the piece. If you

wanted to get technical, a note to H. V. Miller, treasurer of the New York *Herald Tribune*, would bring permission but I consider it unnecessary and would so testify at your trial."

It was Rice who on a Kentucky Derby morning looked at Smith's blood-shot eyes and expressed deep concern. "If you think they look bad, you oughta see 'em from my side," Smith said.

Conversational by-play in a football press box takes funny bounces, too. Surely one of the most uproarious moments in football history came in the 1929 Rose Bowl game between Georgia Tech and University of California when Roy Reigels, California center, picked up a fumble and ran sixty-four yards with the ball—the wrong way! Finally teammate Benny Lom grabbed him, spun him, and right there on the one-yard line he was downed by a Georgia Tech tackler, Frank Waddey. On the field, throughout the stands, up in the press box, everybody's sanity was staggered by the impossible occurrence. The quickest to recover was Zipp Newman of the Birmingham *News*. Turning to his dazed colleagues from Atlanta, New Orleans and Nashville, he clearly and firmly asked this question: "Who was the best second baseman in the Southern League last year?"

I do not know how Zipp got home alive.

On a frigid Thanksgiving Day in 1930, I was seated next to O. B. Keeler in the press box at the Alabama-Georgia game in Birmingham. Since there was no golf to cover at this time of the year, Keeler filled in on football for the Atlanta *Journal*. On this day he was doubly unhappy because he didn't like the idea of working on Thanksgiving, and besides, he was uncomfortable. So O. B. filed this exact one-sentence lead on his running story:

"Legion Field, Birmingham, Ala., Nov. 27——It is ideal football weather, too cold for the players and too cold for the spectators."

Keeler coined his own epigrams. On a festive Cotton Bowl trip, every morning he would shout: "I'm sick and tired of waking up sick and tired." By the time he reached the press box, O. B. had switched to another one: "I am allergic to people who are allergic."

Bill Keefe, writing for the New Orleans *Times-Picayune* for more than forty years, is a character of the Keeler stripe, a true gourmand, salty raconteur and inveterate practical joker. I guess I've made twenty trips with Keefe to Baton Rouge for night football games at Louisiana State University, where the mascot was a very live tiger, Mike. For the games, Mike would be transferred from his permanent concrete and steel-rod home to a portable cage. On all but one of the trips I can account for Keefe's whereabouts immediately after the game. The other time, purely coincidentally, Mike was returned as usual to his secure abode, but the empty portable cage, its door swinging open, was wheeled through town by L. S. U. students asking all who looked their way, and plenty of people of course did, "Have you seen our tiger?"

At the big football games, the night-before and after-game interviews with the coach are now standard procedure for the press boxers. Rarely does any big story develop therefrom, yet most of the newspapermen who were on hand the night before the 1953 Notre Dame-Georgia Tech game thought Frank Leahy was not well. His intimate friend, Julius Tucker of South Bend, at whose home he stayed that night, said later: "I knew the strain Frank was under and I insisted he take some sleeping pills, but he wouldn't do it."

During the game the next day Leahy suffered a physical collapse. When Tucker visited him in the hospital, Leahy told him: "I should have taken your advice about the sleeping pills. I didn't get to sleep until 7:30 in the morning and I was up at 8."

It's possible that Frank Leahy would still be Notre Dame

coach if he had taken the sleeping pills. A few months later I was preparing a story on Leahy's successor, Terry Brennan, for *The Saturday Evening Post,* and after talking to President Theodore N. Hesburgh of Notre Dame I ascertained that Leahy's breakdown in the Georgia Tech game caused the administration to press for his retirement, which otherwise it would not have done.

Football coaches of today give much thought to their choice of words in press conferences. I find this particularly true with such coaches as Jordan Olivar of Yale, Bill Murray of Duke, Tommy Prothro of Oregon State, Sam Boyd of Baylor, Bud Wilkinson of Oklahoma, Ben Martin of Virginia, Andy Pilney of Tulane and Art Guepe of Vanderbilt. Before a recent game Guepe articulated: "We will be striving to get the score beyond the reach of the rather capricious fourth quarter fates." Then, after a defeat: "We are dispirited, but it is not the end of the world. The differential in depth made their victory definite."

A football coach answering questions from a press box delegation after a game must be cautious, lest even his best friends among the sportswriters be tempted to make a funny or devastating retort. When Coach Earl Blaik of Army tried to explain his team's 48-14 defeat by Michigan in 1956 as due almost entirely to the manner in which the Army center handed the ball back to the quarterback, Stanley Woodward, sports editor of the Newark *Star-Ledger* and strictly a Blaik man, said: "Colonel, that's like blaming the Johnstown flood on a leaky toilet in Altoona."

It was the same Woodward, incidentally, who faithfully rehearsed Tony Galento to criticize fellow pugilist Mickey Walker's art paintings in these words: "Your perspective is distorted and the subordination of the motif of composition is vacuous."

In a press box, late in the year, a football writer is not

above composing Christmas verse. Morris McLemore, Miami *Daily News,* did this during time-outs, a probably obvious fact:

> It was the morning of Christmas and all through
> the community,
> Small citizens were stirring, giving no one immunity,
> Large citizens, too, were starry-eyed with fellow-
> ship,
> Their pace much hampered by fruitcake and
> mellowship.

Bert McGrane of the Des Moines *Register and Tribune,* permanent secretary of the Football Writers Association, came up with a new approach in this disturbing poetic thought:

Santa's coming, pack on back, giving reindeers frequent whack, Dancer, Prancer, patience thin, may give Santa kick on shin.

At football and baseball games the press is pampered with drinks and snacks, superb informational and statistical service, and just about everything anybody could think of— or anything everybody could think of. The intentions are honorable, but a fellow must take care. Outside the entrance to the Sugar Bowl stadium not long ago was a blind former boxer who held out his tin cup when he heard people approaching. A man with a portable typewriter came along and as the cup was proffered, he grunted, "Working press."

A sportswriter can develop a one-track mind. Radio and TV people, too. Lindsey Nelson of National Broadcasting Company even while visiting the Colosseum in Rome remained football-conscious, postcarding his friends: "These end zone seats are best. In the old days they could watch the lions play and see the holes open in the Christians."

On occasions I'm asked to single out the most astonishing feat I've watched from a press box. I wish instead someone would ask, "What is the three-fourths most astonishing feat you ever saw, watching a contest from the press box?" That I could answer readily, for it happened on the night of July 19, 1955, in the Southern Association All-Star game at Birmingham.

An overflow crowd of 20,000 stretched down the base lines and spread across the fringe of outfield. On such a spectacular and special occasion I couldn't imagine a man hitting four balls out of the park, even in batting practice. Indeed, I wouldn't have bet that a man could toss up the ball himself ten times and fungo four over the fences. Yet Jim Lemon, rawboned Chattanooga outfielder who graduated to Washington, stepped to the plate against the best pitching the rest of the league could offer and:

Hit a home run into the right-field stands.
Hit one over the left-field fence.
Hit one over the right-field wall.

At this point I made the smart suggestion to Atlanta sportswriters Ed Danforth and Furman Bisher that we had seen about everything, and it would be wise to slip out and grab a taxicab and head for the hotel, beating the crowd. It took almost fifteen minutes to proceed from the roof press box to the street and by the time we were loading into the cab, Lemon was at bat again, in the ninth inning. Things seemed strangely quiet. Then there was a rap—and a crowd roar that told me what a mistake our early departure was. Lemon had done it again, this time into the left-field stands, the kind of clouting exploit that happens once in several lifetimes.

A sportswriter should never leave the press box until the action is over. Even at rowing races, Damon Runyon not only stayed to the end, but in his stories he always had the stroke oar collapsing after crossing the finish line. "It's expected of him," Runyon said, "and my boss likes it."

I wish I wouldn't hurry from the press box, and would

leave leisurely, and not avoid conversations. It was after a Dixie Series baseball game at Houston one night that I heard one of the concession men say, "Peanuts is tension food. People eat peanuts when the score's close and a lot's at stake. That's when they sit tight. When a game is one-sided, or a series ain't important, they eat popcorn. Ice cream, too. They're the stuff that relaxes you. You eat popcorn and ice cream when nothing makes no difference."

Another Dixie Series, between Nashville and San Antonio, brought Bobby Bragan to the press box as a special writer. He had managed Ft. Worth during the season and was experting the series. Newspapermen admire a sports personality who does his own writing, and Bragan exhibited fertile imagination. In a way I regret the dignity Bobby was forced to assume when he moved up to the big leagues as Pittsburgh manager. Around the National League he never became as hated as he would have liked, and he must have missed the razzing he attracted from Texas League fans, and also in the Pacific Coast League when he managed Hollywood.

One night when Bragan's Ft. Worth club was playing Tulsa, his pitcher, Ed Chandler, got into a fight with the Tulsa pitcher, Tommy Warren. In the course of the scuffling, Chandler bit Warren so deeply on the thumb that Warren had to leave the game.

When Bragan walked out on the field the next night, Tulsa fans showered him with meat bones and barked like dogs and seemed to hold him responsible for the bite. Bobby burned quietly. Later in the season, Ft. Worth returned to Tulsa after it had clinched the pennant, and Bragan made a farce of the game. His players tried to steal with the bases loaded, made catches behind their backs and threw the ball into the stands on attempted pickoff plays.

Tulsa fans unloosed a loud chorus of boos and wouldn't quit. The umpires tried to stop them, and couldn't. Finally

Bragan walked out on the diamond and raised his hand for silence. The crowd grew still. Bobby stood there a moment, then suddenly screamed at the top of his voice: "Bow, wow, wow!"

Eddie Stanky when he managed the Cardinals was a visitor in the World Series press box after one of the Yankees-Dodgers games. Chancing upon Roger Kahn, then with the New York *Herald Tribune*, Eddie asked: "How is it that baseball writers who have never managed criticize managers whenever they feel like it?"

Kahn thought it over a moment and replied: "How is it, Eddie, that managers who have never umpired criticize umpires whenever they feel like it?"

But many sportswriters are not critical even when taken out of the press box to fill in as critics on assignments off the sports beat. There was one, you may remember, who covered the symphony concert and wrote: "Wagner's music is better than it sounds."

Sportswriting's Patron Saint

When the Nashville baseball club trained at Baton Rouge in 1942, all trips for exhibition games were made by bus. On the longest jump of the spring, to Shreveport, I drew as a seat-mate a talkative third baseman, Charlie English. After Charlie had chattered about a few dozen places and things, and two hours had elapsed with no chance for snoozing or reading, I attempted to conclude each fresh topic of conversation by remarking, with a tone of finality, "Well, you can't beat that."

Each and every time, English guilelessly countered, "You can't tie it," and kept right on talking. When he would mention a person, I would drone, "You can't beat him," and English, seemingly never conscious of the repetition, would trump, "You can't tie him."

Well, that's how I feel about the late Grantland Rice— you can't tie him. Some of the most rewarding hours of my life have been spent in his company.

Granny was raised in Nashville, graduated at Vanderbilt, worked on Nashville newspapers and returned often up to the time of his mother's death in 1942, at eighty. He was the outstanding man in the history of his profession, and the most beloved; his gift for poetry and prose and his sense of honor and fairness contributed inestimably to the wholesome development of sports in America.

People who should know credit Rice with bringing respectability to sports writing. With his literary talent, he perhaps more than any other lifted it out of the "dese and dose" class. As one veteran put it: "Sports pages popular only in barbershops and pool rooms found their way into more and more homes—by the front door."

All Granny's traits are well known except, possibly, his funny side. I heard him get up at a banquet of horsemen at the Keeneland track at Lexington one night and propose the creation of a 49th state carved out of Middle Tennessee and Central Kentucky, purely Bluegrass.

He, a successor to Walter Camp as selector of All-American football teams for *Collier's* and later *Look,* suggested more than once that a 150-pound team should be picked for *Reader's Digest.*

When some of the newspapermen had to live on houseboats at the 1948 World Series, Granny said: "Cleveland didn't deserve to win the pennant. It had a weak infield—and no hotels."

He could never forget the first time he had Babe Ruth on the radio, and Babe's fracturing of the script, reading a line in this manner: "Duke Ellington once said that the Battle of Waterloo was won on the playing fields of Elkton."

Granny told me the most striking lead he ever saw on a news story was by a Chicago reporter covering a G. A. R. parade in 1912, which began: "God, how their feet hurt!"

To Jack Dempsey, the laughingest line Granny ever turned out was a twisted couplet shortly after Dempsey had won the heavyweight crown from Jess Willard: "Hail the conquering hero comes, surrounded by a bunch of bums."

Rice liked this off-the-cuff philosophic crispie:

> Stone walls do not a prison make?
> Bah! What tommyrot!
> They may not make the prison
> But they help an awful lot.

He thought the cleverest versifying ever submitted to him by a reader was this contribution by Eugene Manlove Rhodes following the 1925 World Series between Pittsburgh and Washington, entitled "The Idyl of Yde":

> Come, gather around me; come, listen and heed,
> To hear the sad story of brave Emil Yde,
> The portsider speedy, of Pittsburgh the pride—
> (And some call him Eedy, and some call him Eyed).
>
> Now Yde was idle until the fourth game—
> (Left-handers don't always shoot quite where they aim).
> Just who to pitch Sunday was hard to decide,
> But Harris tried Johnson, and Pittsburgh tried Yde.
>
> Both idols were busy, for two innings giddy,
> With one walk on Johnson and two upon Yde;
> With two hits on Johnson and one upon Yde,
> And only sharp fielding to hold down the lid.
>
> Third inning—Walt Johnson first up—hit—a bid
> For second—and tagged out! "You're starting to skid!"—
> "Now, Sam Rice, take warning, you mustn't," said Yde,
> "Stretch singles on Pittsburgh . . . Hit this one." . . .
>   He did.
>
> Next play—hard luck, Yde! With a force-out in sight,
> In the moment of need something went wrong with
>   Wright.
> Two runners on base by such fielding untidy,
> Goose Goslin to bat—that's a hard lay for Yde.

194

Now Yde eyed the Goslin, the Goslin eyed Yde,
And the ball came up zipping low down the inside;
The next one was fouled, and the third one was wide—
"BAL-L-L TUH!" bawled the umpire—"Hit this one,"
     said Yde.

Oh, why should the spirit of mortal take pride?
The Goose took a toe-hold, the ball took a ride;
It sailed over Barnhart, it bounded outside!
And that was the end of the idyl of Yde.

(P. S.: The correct pronunciation was Eed-y.)

John Kieran said Granny "put his soul in verse." Sports
and poetry blended perfectly for him. "Rhythm, the main
factor in both, is the main factor in life itself," he used to
say. "Without rhythm, there is a sudden snarl or tangle."

Of all men, I thought Grantland Rice came nearest to
looking the part of a person of ability, decency, compassion,
humor——and a song in his heart. He was a living contradic-
tion to the saying, "Appearances are deceiving." Gene
Fowler named him "The Hat," because of his beaten-up
fedora of Confederate gray. Just as properly he could have
been known as "The Face."

Granny had such ease and well-manneredness that he
would not have seemed out of place in the pulpit——or standing in line to make a daily double bet at the race track.
Henry McLemore called him "an angel with a *Racing Form*
tucked under one wing."

In Granny's last years his favorite spot each March was
Sunshine Park, a cozy and not easily accessible track at
Oldsmar, Florida, about twenty miles equidistant from
Tampa, St. Petersburg and Clearwater. Every spring we
spent at least one afternoon there, usually with Granny's
steadiest traveling companions, Red Smith of the *Herald
Tribune* and Frank Graham of the *Journal-American*. Rice
was no man to take a hand at the steering wheel, and he

195

never bothered to ask the driver which direction he was taking. Whether it was the first or fifteenth trip to Sunshine, if I picked up Granny in front of the Vinoy Park Hotel in St. Petersburg and inquired, "What's the best way to go?", he would answer, invariably, "I have no idea; but somewhere, you cross the Gandy Bridge." And crossing the bridge, Granny usually rhymed some new parody ("Give me a handy guy like Gandy, building a bridge . . . .") of Damon Runyon's memorable verse about jockey Earl Sande.

Rice liked Sunshine because, he explained, there he could get close to the horses, without the melee of the mob. He was completely won by the parking lot attendant's remark, "Not so close to that other car, please. We've got all the room in the world." Also, the astounding statement of the tip-sheet salesman: "The other gentleman just bought one. You're in his party, aren't you? One's enough."

If we were to meet Granny at the track for lunch, there was never any trouble finding him. "Just follow the waiter who has a martini, tomato juice, a dill pickle and Camembert cheese on his tray," Frank Graham would say. Wherever the trail ended, Mr. Rice would be found ingratiating himself to a tout. One day when I joined him he was "martini-ing" and advising with a gentleman who later excused himself, explaining: "It's time for me to go bait my trap." He was the seller in the $10 window.

Granny's weakness was the daily double. He always bought a fistful of tickets. The first time Sunshine honored its most famous booster by naming one race "The Grantland Purse" and another "The Rice Purse," Granny had to present a trophy to a jockey who had just beaten him, by a head, out of a $517.20 double. Which he did, smilingly.

Rice rarely argued with people, and never with machines. Before one of the Philadelphia games of the 1950 World Series he was nursing a heavy cold and Messrs. Graham

196

and Smith suggested that he stay in the hotel suite and watch the game on television. Granny said he didn't know how to work a TV set. They tuned in the channel and left him seated in an easy chair. When they returned after the game, Granny was seated in the same chair watching the same channel, which by then was showing "Howdy Doody." Graham concluded that Granny didn't know how to turn off the set, but Smith explained: "No, he was just too polite. He was afraid he would hurt the actors' feelings."

One of the few times Rice was embarrassed was when the fellow writer he was riding with in Florida had a puncture, and Granny, knowing only that an automobile had four wheels, was of no help. While waiting, he decided the least thing he could do would be to spread some newspapers for his companion to kneel on while changing the tire. In so doing, he accidentally kicked the hub-cap containing the lugs into the roadside canal.

Among the most enjoyable appurtenances of sportswriting are the opportunities to laugh with one's colleagues over the shenanigans they haven't seen fit, for one reason or another, to incorporate in their columns. In the late 1930's, I think Granny got most of his laughs from Henry McLemore, then writing for the United Press and now with McNaught Syndicate. Any time they visited Nashville, there had to be one very special lunch of ham-and-biscuit and jam-and-biscuit, wrapped in grease-spotted newspaper, just like country school.

As Granny's golfing partner, Henry once spewed his first tee shot just a few yards down the fairway. "I have a hen," he exclaimed, "who can lay an egg farther than that."

When the 1937 Alabama team played California in the Rose Bowl, Rice and McLemore invited some of the Southern newspapermen to a party at the home of the late Guy Kibbee, of the movies. Driving home afterward through

197

fog and Los Angeles' easy-to-lose-your-way canyons, Henry decided to stick close behind the tail-light of another car. He was doing all right until the car in front suddenly stopped and McLemore banged into its rear end. Incensed, Henry jumped out, demanding, "Why didn't you hold out your hand?"

"In my own garage?" said the bumped-into gentleman.

One time Rice, McLemore and Kibbee were visiting their friend Clarence Budington Kelland in Arizona. The idea was to play golf and rest, but upon arrival McLemore learned that a half-mile race track was in operation in a nearby town. He couldn't pass that up, nor could Kibbee.

Early afternoon found them at the little track, where the dust was fetlock deep and the infield was cluttered with cottonwood trees. Their presence was soon discovered in the small audience. Indeed, within a few minutes bugles were sounded and from the judges' stand it was announced via the loud-speaker that the track was honored by the visit of the two distinguished guests.

They were taken over to a box seat to meet an official of the track, a gentleman with a big hat, a long cigar and a friendly voice. After introductions and exchanges of greetings, Mr. Kibbee inquired in a dulcet tone if the official of the track would be so kind as to mark their program.

"My friend," he whispered to Kibbee, "the sixth race is fixed. Don't ask me any questions. But you may ignore every other race and wait for the sixth. No. 3 is the horse. Go as far as you like."

Kibbee and McLemore stumbled over each other in their hurry from the box, thinking they would phone Rice and Kelland. No, they decided they would bet for them. For years they had waited for such a day. Imagine, a fixed race! A sure thing!

They smiled their way through the first five races, exchanging knowing glances, refusing to wager a penny, refusing even to buy cigarets, for every penny was going on No. 3 in the sixth. They loaded up.

As the horses paraded to the post, McLemore was staggered to see the size of the jockey on No. 3. He was about six feet tall; the others were midgets. He and Kibbee rushed back to the box of the kindly official who had passed along the tip. The gentleman reassured them, in hurried whispers, that this was a part of it. Then they scrambled to get a view of the start of the race. Kibbee looked through his field glasses, then handed them to McLemore, saying painfully, "Do you see what I see?"

"The jockey had clutched in his right hand an enormous piece of stove wood," Henry tells it. "He raised it over the head of the horse. Then, just as they all broke from the barrier, he brought it down with all his might on our No. 3's cranium. The horse's legs crumbled under him. He went to the ground. He got up and went to the ground again. Finally he got up and staggered around the track 400 yards behind the others. We fell over backward ourselves. We finally got up and ran to the box seats to see our great and good friend. He was gone. We sat down and had a good cry."

Rice had his full share of fun while turning out millions of words covering all the top events. No sportswriter before or since established as many contacts or enjoyed as many confidences. In his company, coaches and managers and athletes relaxed, never feeling they had to be cautious in what they said.

On the day after the 1943 Army-Navy game, I was with Granny, Frank Graham and Capt. John E. Whelchel, the Navy coach, at the Chatham Hotel in New York. Whelchel related one of the most fantastic football recruiting feats I ever heard, requesting that nothing be written about it until he was through coaching. It would have been a sensational story then, and subsequent events have made it well worth telling now.

Planning for that 1943 season in August, Whelchel had mentioned to E. E. (Rip) Miller, assistant athletic director at Navy and the Academy's chief procurer of talent, his desperate need for a tackle. Miller at the time happened to be thumbing through a just-published copy of *Illustrated Football Annual,* which was filled with pictures of the players of the previous season.

The two discussed the situation and then made a sudden and most extraordinary decision: they would choose from the magazine the tackle with the fiercest face.

Through close study, they picked Don Whitmire, who had played in 1942 at University of Alabama.

What to do next? They sent for Bobby Tom Jenkins, who had played halfback at Alabama before transferring to Navy. Did Jenkins know Whitmire?

Jenkins certainly did. In fact, they had been roommates at Tuscaloosa.

Did he think Whitmire might be interested in an appointment to the Naval Academy?

"I would say yes," Jenkins answered. "Right now he's at the North Carolina Preflight School, I think."

At Miller's direction Jenkins telephoned Whitmire. Don jumped at the chance. But the Alabama Senators and Congressmen had no appointments left.

Miller handled that pronto. A swap was made and a member of the House of Representatives from Illinois who had not used his appointments sent Whitmire to Annapolis.

And the best part of the story is that Whitmire proved such an excellent leader that later he was elected Navy's team captain, remained in the service and today is recog-

200

nized as a splendid officer having spent duty first aboard destroyers and later in submarines.

Nothing pleased Rice more than to see players he selected as All-Americans develop into outstanding career men. He liked to talk to a boy off the field before he made his final choice. He almost leaned over backward in preventing friendship or sentiment from influencing his decision; through all the years he picked only one player from Vanderbilt—the captain and center, Carl Hinkle, in 1937. Hinkle in the game against Tennessee that year gave the most rousing final-five-minutes performance by a lineman that I've ever witnessed. Vanderbilt was trying to hang on to a 13-7 lead as Tennessee tore into its territory ripping off long gains. Within four plays, linebacker Hinkle's murderous tackles sent ball-carriers Cheek Duncan and George Cafego to the sidelines as Tennessee was stopped at the nine-yard line. Vanderbilt punted out and then, as a game-ending clincher, Hinkle intercepted a pass. Later at West Point, where he became the No. 1 cadet, Hinkle was ineligible for further collegiate football but he scrimmaged frequently against the varsity. Today he is an Air Force colonel in the intelligence branch of SHAPE, stationed in Paris.

Grantland Rice died July 13, 1954, at seventy-three. Two months before, he, Bill Corum and I had met at Toots Shor's for lunch. We were still there at five o'clock. Shor idolized Rice. "On your seventy-fifth birthday," Toots told Granny, "I'm throwing you the finest party that's ever been thrown." Which he did, but on the day that would have been Rice's seventy-fourth birthday, November 1, 1954. All Granny's friends were there, and before the evening was over sportswriter Cas Adams was laying 8 to 5 that Granny himself would show up—and getting no takers.

Perhaps the testimonial paid Granny the Sunday night preceding the party at Shor's indicated in what respect he was held by those in all walks of life who had come to know him as a typewriter-bearing angel. That Sunday night Ed Sullivan's *Toast of the Town* hour devoted thirty valuable minutes of its program to the life of Granny and his posthumous autobiography, *The Tumult and the Shouting*, which was published the following day. Jack Dempsey, the fabulous Four Horsemen, Gene Sarazen, Eddie Arcaro, Vinnie Richards and Johnny Weismuller were some of the giants of sport who paraded before the cameras to tell of the feeling and love they held for Granny. Tribute indeed when a nationwide TV show, hemmed in by inflating production costs, thinks enough of a sportswriter to hold a thirty-minute tribute.

The dinner was attended by just about everyone who knew Granny, and who was able to appear. Actually John Lowell Pratt, publisher of Granny's autobiography, planned on the dinner to launch the publicity campaign of the book and he had already made provisions for the costs in his promotion budget. The dinner over, Lowell asked Toots for the tab for the more than 400 guests. Toots informed the publisher that the party was his, Toots', and "nobody else's." Lowell insisted this wasn't so and started to argue with Toots, being stopped only when Shor placed his ample right hand on Lowell's left shoulder.

"Listen, Lowell," rasped Toots. "You run your book business and let me run my saloon." So Toots picked up the tab, a not too insignificant amount, either, considering that the guests were men of tremendous thirst and hearty appetite.

The Thoroughbred Racing Associations, adopting a suggestion by Bill Corum, established at Vanderbilt the TRA-Grantland Rice Memorial Scholarship, one of the most generous grants ever offered, for students "who are the likeliest prospects in America to become fine sportswriters."

"Grantland Rice was the greatest man I have known, the

greatest talent, the greatest gentleman," wrote Red Smith. "The most treasured privilege I have had in this world was knowing him and going about with him as his friend. I shall be grateful all my life."

Someone once said: "He's greatest who's most often in men's good thoughts."

Writing A Column

I've written close to 8,500 sports columns without ever doing one I thought couldn't be better. That's why I keep dreaming how nice it would be to be—well, a postman. How reassuring to put letters into a mail box and know that no human being in the world, no matter how talented or experienced, could do that job any better! You either place the letter in the right box—or you don't. You perform the task to the highest degree of excellence, or you fail completely; there's no in between.

The sports columnist almost never knows for sure how well or how poorly he has done. I gotta tote dat bale without ever learning what the thing weighs.

Sometimes, just because it's such a change, I derive a queer pleasure from simply writing a check. At least some of the pain of paying out is alleviated by the knowledge that I'm wording something perfectly and conclusively. That is, unless it bounces.

A blank piece of paper in a typewriter is a frightening thing to a sports columnist until he becomes accustomed to his peculiar way of earning a living. He tries awfully hard to have the framework of his essay in mind before seating himself for the business of hitting the right typewriter keys.

There are, however, some gifted exceptions—among them Bill Corum of the New York *Journal-American*, Bill Cunningham of the Boston *Herald,* Ned Cronin of the Los Angeles *Times* and Vincent X. Flaherty of the Los Angeles *Examiner* —who can start a column never knowing for sure where the next paragraph is coming from, or what it's going to be about, and glide gracefully through a word-waltz. Cunningham hits the bass keys more often, packing a little thunder in his pieces, but never losing step.

I have most of my trouble with the first line and the first paragraph of a column. At the start, I'm always pedaling uphill. Once I'm satisfied that the first two or three paragraphs are acceptable, the rest comes easier.

When writing something special, such as a piece to offer *The Saturday Evening Post,* I used to make sure to work at least one semicolon into the first paragraph. Somehow I figured it impressed on the editors that I knew what I was doing. Then one year I crowded a semicolon, a colon and a dash into the lead paragraph of "Pigskin Preview" for the *Post* and got three separate remonstrances, one from Robert Fuoss, semicolon editor; another from Marty Sommers, colon editor, and still another from Harry Paxton, dash editor.

This ended my one conscious effort to give any particular style to my writing. Maybe my stuff has a style, maybe not; I leave the question to the reader, since the rule I follow rather hopefully is the old one that says "Take care of the sense and let the style take care of itself."

Everything the columnist sees or hears or thinks about— everything that happens to him—is possible material from which he composes his 800-to-1,000 words. A columnist is both helped and bedeviled by his almost unlimited choice of things to write about. Often there's the urge to throw away the lead and start all over on another subject. Sometimes I succumb, but not until I've tested myself by asking, "Does a farmer plant a field and then plough up the seeds?" Once in a while I have to tell myself, "This here farmer has just learned he's planted sorry seeds"—and rip the paper out of the machine.

Even when the subject is absolutely settled, as when covering an event such as the World Series or one of the major golf tournaments, there's always a decision to make on what's the best column approach.

If I've assigned a staff reporter to do a straight news story on a sports event, I make sure not to invade his territory with what I write in the column. The responsibility for avoiding duplication rests with the column writer. Yet, even in good newspapers today you stumble over repetitions, which occur in the haste of getting out editions following a big football game.

On most newspapers outside of New York, Boston and Chicago, the man who is sports editor is also the paper's main sports columnist. In recent years a good many papers, including mine, have seen fit to create the position of executive sports editor or sports managing editor, taking some of the load off the department head and giving him more time for columning. But more time for columning is not the same as all the time; he is far from completely free of the worries and duties of sports editor, and he's apt to think, in his moments of self-pity, what a snap those fellows have who just write a column and send it in. The pure sports columnist, unless in a press box or traveling, does most of his writing at home, dropping by the office only to pick up the mail and his paycheck.

Home isn't necessarily an ideal place for writing. We have four daughters. When Kay, Ellen, Lee and Carolyn were younger, and before we built an upstairs den into which I could retreat, I once was obliged to honor their lively, interruptive presence in a volume of sports humor, dedicating it to them—"who made this book practically impossible." I'm the man who tried in vain to get our county school board to add to the curriculum a new course, "Domestic Silence."

I suppose every writer has his own notion of what's the most vexatious distraction. I have done my work under all kind of conditions at ball games and prize fights and fox hunts. They offer no noise or inconvenience that derails my train of thought like a motor bike or piano practice shattering the stillness of home. And the telephone; on a per ring basis and volume of conversation, at our house I guess it's the world's greatest bargain. I figure the monthly cost is about three-thousandths of a mill per word. I've arrived at another statistical conclusion: the chance of a phone's being answered promptly when no one is in the house is almost as good as when six people are there.

At a newspaper office, visitors to the editorial department sometimes marvel at the reporters and editors and columnists being able to do their work amid such varied activity, where desks adjoin, the noise is steady and the traffic heavy. In such surroundings, concentration is possible only because it is habitual: the writer mentally withdraws into his own isolation booth. And no newspaperman is tolerated very long on a staff if he's a loud and incessant talker. In fact, I know of no trait that detracts from able and otherwise attractive persons, whatever their pursuit, as does clamorous talk. Fishermen are a quiet breed, yet they were chosen to be apostles.

A room or roomette on a train is a good place to write a column, best of all when it's raining or snowing outside. In a newspaperman's world, it's difficult to achieve the luxury of occasional total solitude. I suspect this is increasingly true of everybody in today's crowded civilization. Not long ago I rode a train from Chicago to Los Angeles and near the end of the trip it suddenly dawned on me that in forty-three hours I had said no more than thirty words, and those to the Pullman porter and dining car waiters. It was wonderful.

It was wonderful simply because it was such a change. It's nice to take time now and again to make your own acquaintance, to meet yourself. But the sportswriter who prefers to be alone often, who doesn't like people, is in the wrong business. A sportswriter's problem is to balance the discipline of work, worthwhile reading and self-examination against sociability. Without the latter he is minus the personal contacts from which much information, stimulating comment, opinions and thoughts are obtained. Nevertheless, there are times when a writer is much tempted by the advice Christopher Morley included in a tribute to Don Marquis:

"Energy is not endless, better hoard it for your own work. Be intangible and hard to catch, be secret and proud and inwardly unconformable. Say yes and don't mean it; pretend to agree; dodge every kind of organization, and evade, elude, recede. Be about your affairs, as you would also forbear from others at theirs, and thereby show your respect for the holiest ghost we know, the creative imagination."

Some literary analysts think the most important single quality a writer must have is empathy. They describe empathy as, basically, the ability to get inside another person and see things through his eyes. "Sympathy is feeling *for* someone else," says Sydney Harris. "Empathy is feeling *with* them." But right or wrong, I write my column for myself. I express my own notions and thoughts. When I describe or report something that I have seen or heard, I consciously strive to interest and inform the man I would be if I had not been present. If I spent my time trying to imagine what other people would like best to read, I wouldn't have time left to write. I think the first principle of writing is to make the idea interesting to me. It's probably true that, once established in a regular position in a newspaper, a columnist is read not so much for his material as for his view of it.

For form and fashion, a sports columnist can take lessons from some of the games he follows so closely. A baseball pitcher may have a lot on his fast ball but if he throws this same pitch all the time, the batters come to know what to expect and this sameness will beat him. To win, the pitcher mixes his fast ball with curves and a change of pace. So does the columnist who throws words and sentences and hopes to be read regularly.

The never-ending quest is for fresh ideas and fresh words. Rather, combinations of words. Much of the time, dictionary accuracy is inadequate for expressing what the writer wants to say; there are words that dance and there are words that must be wallflowers.

Expressive words characterize the columns of Red Smith, and are solid reasons for the wide and devoted following he has acquired in his twelve years on the *Herald Tribune*. He has a special and piquant propensity for agreeable collective nouns. "No matter how familiar people may be with words," Smith once wrote, "most people are obscurely pleased to be reminded that when Moby Dick was among friends he helped make up a gam of whales; that several fur coats at play constitute a pod of seals; that a flock of geese at rest are a gaggle of geese.

"We have, too, a yard of deer, an exaltation of larks, a shoal of fish, a pride of lions, a farrow of pigs, a hatch of flies, a span of mules, a herd of antelopes and a bevy of broads."

Mr. Smith also registered sporting terms of his own invention, such as a gangle of basketball players, a yammer of radio announcers, a prevarication of golfers, a vagrance of tennis players, a braille of umpires, a flatulence of educators and, guiltily, an indigence of writers.

Some words are spongy with flavor, and blessed is the writer with the knack of diving and coming up with them. Such as Jimmy Cannon's line: "Beer drinkers lead a dreary and gaseous existence." Or vivid descriptives, as Garry Schumacher's: "Florida is shaped like an umpire's thumb."

There was a Southern fullback whose combination of power and elusiveness prompted his coach to depict him as "a cross between a wild bull and a hummingbird."

I remember a conversation with the late John H. Sorrells, a Scripps-Howard executive, early in 1938 before he and Frank Ahlgren, editor of the Memphis *Commercial Appeal,* lured Walter Stewart back from New York to be sports editor. "The written word is a drop of acid that bites deep," Sorrells said. "I like words that sometimes gallop, and always have feel, and texture, and smell, and color, and taste and sound."

When Ed Danforth retired in February, 1957, after nearly forty years as an Atlanta sportswriter, he exhibited his quick eye, penetrating mind and way with words in recapturing assorted memories: ". . . tall pines rolling with the punch of a storm . . . watermelon heart, cold . . . field hand singing wordless blues as he rides the mule toward the barn at night . . . whine of a spinning saw as it bites into an oak log . . . frogs playing saxophones at sundown . . . slim silver moon guarded by a single star."

I think the most skillful writing is that which provides the fullest and most graphic picture in the fewest words. A recent gem was a *New Yorker* reporter's four-word characterization of a mob of Elvis Presley fans as "young, loud, soiled, incoherent."

Arthur Daley of the New York *Times* chanced to be in my office at the *Banner* on the May afternoon in 1956 when he received a telephone call that he had won a Pulitzer Prize. He gasped, and was speechless for several seconds. Pressed for comment, he said: "Just describe my condition as 'stunned delight.' "

Most sports columnists read so much and hear so much and write so much that they never can be certain as to what is incontestably original. Which, actually, doesn't make a lot of difference. Nobody owns words. Who knows who *first* said anything? "What matters," says Professor Roscoe Ellard of Columbia University, "is who said it *best*." If a writer is smitten with the sudden high-voltage idea that world-wide nudism would be the greatest force for peace, inasmuch as without uniforms warring nations wouldn't know whom to shoot at, he should propose it promptly. Or if he gives birth to a paraphrase such as, "Nothing exceeds like excess," he shouldn't refrain from using it for fear of prior coinage.

What a writer should fear is triteness. The suggestion has been made of a five-day week for overworked words, and there was a Chicago editor who decreed: "What this newspaper needs is some new cliches." I would be inclined to vote for the first politician who, just to be different, called something a "political volleyball."

It is a fact that one of the best sports editors of our time demoted an otherwise excellent sportswriter, as it turned out, for the crime of permitting that ancient character, Jupe Pluvius, to slip into his account of a rained-out baseball game.

Some of the worst cliches of the sports page deserve putting into catechism form:

Q—What are the bowl football games?
A—Annual classics.
Q—Who are the people who will pay to see these games?
A—Cash customers.

Q—If one team is superior, how much superior?
A—Vastly.
Q—With what kind of fury does a team strike?
A—With pent-up fury.
Q—When do you see the results on the scoreboard?
A—When the smoke of battle has cleared.
Q—If the winning team had some players injured, what kind of victory was it?
A—A costly victory.
Q—What did the winning coach do?
A—He sang the praises of his team.
Q—To what extent?
A—To the high heavens.
Q—Did anyone smile on his team?
A—Yes. Dame Fortune.
Q—What kind of effort did our boys make?
A—Herculean.
Q—What kind of maneuvers did the opposing team employ?
A—Intricate.
Q—When our team recovered a couple of fumbles and intercepted a pass or two, what do you say?
A—The team was alert.
Q—Now that our boys have come through thus far unbeaten, what is it about them that remains clean?
A—Their escutcheon.

Most writers would get into very little trouble by just writing as they talk. Have you ever heard anybody actually *speak* the word "gridiron" in reference to a football field— or "horsehide" or "hardwood" or "pellet" or "gonfalon?"

People, too, can become cliches if a columnist isn't careful. What I mean is, I think I could take the most popular man in town and merely by mentioning him in my column every few days, even in a consistently flattering manner, I could make him one of the most unpopular, for readers bore easily and resent that which bores them. If they reach the point where they can anticipate approximately what and who the columnist is going to write about, that newspaper should be looking for a new columnist.

Readers love to catch sportswriters in mistakes, in errors of fact and of judgment. Credit human nature for this fondness for seeing the so-called expert fall flat on his face. I covered the first Joe Louis-Max Schmeling fight in 1936 and predicted that the unbeaten Louis would quickly flatten the washed-up German. Instead, Schmeling knocked out Louis in twelve rounds. The next few days my mail was about fifteen times heavier than normal. On the other hand, my mail increased scarcely at all when I picked the 1955 Kentucky Derby finish 1-2-3, and one of the letters was from a fellow who said I couldn't do it again for the Preakness.

The sports page audience is remarkably well informed. You can bet that inaccuracy in a column, involving anything from archery to zebra racing, will be spotted. Misinformation which appears in type isn't forgotten nearly so quickly as those mistakes of the spoken word. Weeks later, letters may remind the author of his guilt.

Oddly, and perhaps fortunately, very few columnists have secretaries. Most of them let the mail accumulate and try to answer it about once a week. Ludwig Bemelmans, the playwright and painter, may have the best system—three rubber stamps and a pad. He returns every letter to the sender stamped in one of three categories:

If highly complimentary—I LOVE YOU, I LOVE YOU
If mildly critical—GO SEE A DOCTOR
If extremely bitter—ADDRESS UNKNOWN.

Writing A Column Every Damn Day

In 1946 a plane loaded with sportswriters was approaching Lexington to see the running of the Bluegrass Stakes at Keeneland. A severe thunderstorm delayed the landing. The plane circled in the dark clouds, then suddenly made a pass at the airport.

"I don't think we'll make it," said Harry Grayson, outspoken sports editor of the NEA Service, chewing on his unlit half-cigar.

"Well, if we don't, there's one consolation," said Grantland Rice.

"What?" Grayson asked.

"Won't have to write any column tomorrow," Granny explained, never changing his expression.

Tomorrow hangs always over the head of the daily sports columnist. After one column is finished, only a deep sigh separates the start of a new chain of thought on what to write about the next day.

Budd Schulberg, author of five successful books in a row, wrote a column for a weekly magazine for a year, then quit. "I had to give it up," he said. "I always had that

214

thing hanging over my head. I couldn't get if off my mind."

Deadlines confront the newspaper columnist six days a week. His piece has to be finished by a certain time. If it doesn't jell, he can't chuck it and say, "I'll try again later." He has to do it, somehow, now.

"The most awful sound in the world," said Fred Schwed, Jr., "is the typewriter when it's not going."

There's a story, not new, about the frantic fellow at his machine who had twenty minutes left, then ten, then five, who in desperation grabbed the scissors, snatched an out-of-town newspaper and cut hurriedly therefrom, pasting the clipping on a piece of copy paper under the quickly-typed sentence, "I wonder what Walter Lippman means by this?"

While that may sound unduly exigent, it's not much worse than the occasional practice of busy law judges in higher courts rendering a verdict of a case on appeal and adopting in toto the written opinion of the lower court.

My column, being in an afternoon newspaper, has to be in the hands of the copy editor by eight-thirty each morning. No matter where I go or what I do or how late I stay up, those three to four typewritten pages must be brought, sent, mailed, telegraphed or telephoned to the office by 8:30 A.M. Most of the time, when in Nashville, I'm at the office myself by then, checking to see if I should add anything to the column or perhaps put a "top" on it. I will have written it the morning or afternoon or night before, depending upon the circumstances. Always, even when I'm on an out-of-town assignment, I can wire or phone a new lead or add a section before eight-thirty, and, for the main edition, as late as noon. When the occasion seems to demand it, home or road, I get up at 6 A.M. and write a complete new column for the day, pushing the already-written stuff ahead to the next day and hoping it won't spoil. The fact that fully half such displaced columns do spoil beyond use in twenty-four hours testifies to the unpredictability of news.

Personally, I think there are too many days in the week. There should be six instead of seven. I would throw out Tuesdays, and take those twenty-four hours and slice them six ways and add four hours to each of the other days. Then we would have six 28-hour days, more time for everybody to play or rest or do whatever they want to do, and yet retain the same 144-hour week. I'm unashamedly selfish in this proposal; with those extra four hours a day, a columnist might be able to always carry a "spare."

A few writers do try to build up a column bank from time to time. It's easiest to do this in baseball spring training, but even then the margin is thin, seldom exceeding more than two or three days. There was a prolific Detroit journalist who once confessed to being eighteen days ahead in his columns. "Cripes!" exclaimed a horrified colleague. "Suppose you died and got stuck with them?"

I write some columns in advance, when there's minimum risk of their going stale. I would like to do it more often, but it's next to impossible when so much is going on in sports every day and I'm trying to keep up with it.

Timing is everything. It dictates what to write about. On the day of the bowl football games I would hardly speculate on U.S. Davis Cup tennis prospects or argue either way on the question of baseball's reserve clause. In fact, of all the lessons sports teaches which can be applied to life and living, timing may be the most important.

Know how to make a sorry meal taste better? Postpone it about an hour and a half.

Know how to make money in the stock market? Just find out when's the time to buy and when to sell.

Charlie Dressen told me he thought a mistake in timing cost him the Brooklyn baseball managership when he resigned in 1953 after the Dodgers had extended him a one-year contract. "It was five-thirty in the afternoon when I sprang it on Walter O'Malley (Brooklyn owner) that I

216

wanted a three-year contract," Dressen said. "He was just leaving to keep a dinner engagement. It upset him. If I had broached the matter at nine-thirty in the morning, things might have worked out different. That taught me a lesson; a man should handle all his important business before lunch."

Cleverest timing stunt I ever witnessed was pulled by a friendly and informative old Negro guide at Silver Springs, Florida, one of nature's showplaces near Ocala. The glass-bottomed boat, filled with passengers, was gliding into the dock as another tour was about to end. "Now, if you folks will look straight down," said the conductor, "you will see one of the biggest kingfish in the world."

As all eyes peered downward, the guide slipped a quarter from his own pocket and flipped it into the air so that it landed loudly at his own feet.

"Thank you, suh!" he exclaimed, tipping his hat to the phantom benefactor. "Thank you very much, suh!"

Thus prompted, the tourists gave him a small cascade of coins.

I knew a mercurial columnist who, on the day his newspaper was conducting a survey to determine its best-read features, roofed his epistle with the eye-catching caption, "I Hate To Break A Confidence, But—"

A sense of timing can make a prayer especially unforgettable. The instance I remember best was the invocation at the American College Baseball Coaches Association dinner in St. Louis in January, 1957, by the Reverend Wilfred H. Crowley, S. J., University of Santa Clara, who said, in part:

> May we who teach a game played on what is called a diamond be given the grace to develop jewels of the spirit, such as honesty, loyalty and courage.
>
> Grant that in a sport that counts the score at home, we may be ever mindful of our heavenly

217

home, while teaching on the field of play the things that will make the youth of today worthy fathers in the homes of America.

May we who direct the skills of men in a game that uses the tactic called a sacrifice build up the moral fiber that can join the will to win with self-discipline and fair play, and impart the wisdom to understand that the true satisfaction of life consists in giving rather than getting.

Time, as well as timing, is essential to most columnists. I rarely work fast. It usually takes me about an hour and thirty minutes to do a piece, not counting preliminary procrastinating, of which I am not overly guilty. I don't smoke. I don't whistle. I don't sharpen eight or ten pencils. I don't make trips to the water fountain when I get stalled, although this habit worked well for my first sports editor boss, Ralph Perry. I'm just a starer at the paper in the typewriter, a looker-out-of-the-window, and an x-outer of what has been written that doesn't please me, though for latter purpose the "m" key serves me just as faithfully as the "x". I'm not superstitious, but at home I use the same portable typewriter I bought in 1932; it does all right.

I've never learned the touch system of typing because with the two-finger method I still can type faster than I can think. I don't know more than a half-dozen sportswriters who are rapid all-finger typists: Bob Considine of International News Service; Wilfrid Smith, Chicago *Tribune;* Bob Phillips, Birmingham *Post-Herald* and Tom Anderson, Knoxville *Journal.* Anderson, who spent his first years in sportswriting on our staff at the *Banner,* was the fastest writer I ever saw—and the author of some brilliant pieces done at stenographic speed.

Westbrook Pegler, a painstaking hard-hitting craftsman as a sportswriter in what he termed the Era of Wonderful Nonesense following World War I, might spend four hours on a column. It was Pegler who said: "In a given number of turns at bat, a columnist must have those days when he is a wooden Indian, never getting his bat off his shoulder, and those days when he grounds out miserably to the pitcher or pops a high foul."

While no less an authority than William Faulkner is convinced that good whisky is an aid to enticing the muse, I now rarely see a newspaperman drinking in working hours. There was a time, back in prohibition days twenty-five and more years ago, when the stuff was rather commonplace around newspaper offices. I knew many brethren who couldn't—or didn't—start a column before taking a charge. Today few newspapermen try to mix drink with writing. H. L. Mencken gave what I think was the best advice: "Never drink if you have any work to do. Never drink alone. Even if you haven't got any work to do, never drink while the sun is shining. Wait until it's dark."

The Motlow brothers, who operate the oldest registered distillery in the United States at little Lynchburg, Tennessee, take witty cognizance of the cocktail hour by wearing special wristwatches on which every numeral is a 5. The Motlows have been friends of mine since college days, and if I could truthfully testify that I have found sports columns in their black-labeled bottles I would gladly do so. Relaxation from columns, but no columns. Pleasant dreams, but no words to describe them.

I'm at my best, I think, after mild exercise, a shower and a body rubdown. Some of the column ideas I've liked the most came to mind on the masseur's table. A rubdown is the most relaxing thing in the world for me, and I try to get two a week.

There's nothing that puts me in a better humor than capturing a notion for a column sorta accidentally, or without great effort. If a press agent is sharp enough to foresee a dull columnar day, and can make his blurb validly amusing or informative, I won't pass it up simply because he has an angle. Indeed, almost everyone is promoting something or other. If world traveler Abe Saperstein has eyes and ears for what's unusual, I won't disqualify him because he works something in about his Harlem Globetrotters.

I'm grateful to anyone—especially the purveyors of humor who pass along what might afford me a holiday. Tim Cohane, sports editor of *Look*, does it each September; I'm Southern distributor for his "Bull Pond All-American Football Team," comically illustrated by ingenious cartoonist Willard Mullin, who also serves as the team psychiatrist. It recently heralded such stellar performers as Lancelot Longhand of King Arthur's Knight School, Heinrich Schnorkel of Unterwasser U., Lafcadio Jaggedrazor of Bedlam Hall, Wolfgang Mucker of Sadistic Tech and Ferdinand Fraud of Harvard Business.

As an occasional columnar change of pace, I employ the services of a fictitious character named Stagnant, said to make his home in a hammock under a bridge spanning the Cumberland River in Nashville, who has been known to prophesy the outcome of sports events by reading what the dandelions spell out when dropped into a steaming cauldron of equal parts of hyena milk and donkey sweat.

Fastest columns I do are conversation pieces. There was a time, when baseball players were more colorful characters than today's minor-leaguers, that I could visit the Nashville dugout before a game and seldom fail to land a column. Sometimes it was accomplished with the collusion of two or three chatty players who would sense the situation and promote discussion of a subject or a personality. These quotes didn't necessarily have to make much sense just as long as they were authentic. I remember one day in 1940 when the Birmingham club was taking batting practice and

I, sitting on the Nashville bench, remarked that Mike Dejan, Birmingham outfielder, certainly could hit the ball a long way. This conversation ensued:

JOHN MIHALIC—"Yes, he has a lot of power, as much as anybody in the league."
ORIS HOCKETT—"What nationality is he, French?"
BOB BOKEN—"No, he's a Pole."
MIHALIC—"I know one thing, he was born in Canada."
BOOTS POFFENBERGER—"That's tough."
MIHALIC—"Why? What's tough about it?"
POFFENBERGER—"He can never be President."

Seven or eight snatches like that one and I had a quick column.

The finest ear for conversation and fidelity of recreating it on paper exactly as it was said belongs, I think, to Frank Graham, the mild little man of the New York *Journal-American*. He never takes a note; no longer is this a novelty among newspapermen, but Graham with his axiomatic accuracy can hemstitch pretty pieces out of everyday small talk by athletes.

Most managers and coaches, as well as players, will talk freely to sportswriters they like and trust. They tell an awful lot to John Carmichael of the Chicago *Daily News*. Day in and day out, his column carries the liveliest quotes and opinions. Carmichael never probes or crusades; he seeks and captures what's significant, humorous or unusual, and travels so extensively that he's in Chicago little more than half the year. Other writers who maintain exceptionally fruitful contacts, although based outside major league territory, are Tom Siler, Knoxville *News-Sentinel;* Sec Taylor, Des Moines *Register and Tribune;* Furman Bisher, Atlanta *Journal;* and Clark Nealon, Houston *Post.*

When Tom Meany was on the staff of the New York

World-Telegram and later the tabloid *PM,* he had the widest and warmest acquaintance with other sportswriters throughout the nation. Such relationships are invaluable to columnists. The surest way to get the inside story or the freshest angle or the funniest slant on any sudden development in sports is to telephone your best friend in the place where it happened.

Worst mistake a paper can make is to chain to a desk a sunny soul who thrives on conviviality and who can turn talk and tips into good copy. Long years ago, Bill Keefe served time as city editor on the *Times-Picayune.* He hated the job's confining requirements, and concocted a way out. Bill's scheme was exceedingly simple. He kept an extra hat and coat at the office, hidden away, which he wore on quick visits to his favorite New Orleans haunts while the coat-rack in the city room proclaimed—or seemed to—that he had only gone as far as the washroom or the composing room or the photo department.

All columnists strive for a balanced schedule of subject matter. Even at the peak of the football season, they'll think twice before writing about football three days in a row. In this respect the syndicated columnist has the biggest problem, trying to satisfy clients in all parts of the country. But the truth is that after Grantland Rice's death the syndicated sports column was just about passé, because most newspapers were depending on their own men. It's not unusual now for a paper to carry one local sports column on the first sports page and another on the second. The Los Angeles *Times* actually has five sports columnists; Ned Cronin appears every day, sports editor Paul Zimmerman alternates with Braven Dyer, and Dick Hyland alternates with Frank Finch. I've never ascertained for sure how they avoid conflicts and duplication on subject matter.

Red Smith revived the syndicated sports column. He's so good that newspapers will buy him, even if they haven't the space to use him more than twice a week, just to keep their competition from grabbing him.

Smith thinks New York is the easiest place in America to write a sports column. "All you need is a good pair of legs—or taxi fare," he says. "There's so much going on." Certainly New York is dead as a football town, and it has been losing some of the big fights to other cities, but always it reeks with extraordinary sports personalities, both resident and transient.

I believe a writer could set up shop in Toots Shor's Restaurant on 51st Street and turn out a sprightly column every day. All he would need is a tape recorder. If I'm going to New York and want to see some friends in the sports crowd, I don't have to phone them; I know they'll be dropping into Shor's. The Football Writers Association meets there for lunch every Monday during the fall. In baseball season, it's only 12 to 15 minutes from the Polo Grounds and Yankee Stadium by subway. It's just across the street from the Associated Press offices, where many sportswriters visiting New York write their pieces. Toots uses no tricks in attracting the sports, theatrical and newspaper people into his place; I think the main lure is that he personifies that common desire of so many Americans to know sports celebrities intimately. Many wealthy men attempt to buy the same privilege and can't get to first base because they're either oversolicitous or bores. Toots is unfeigned, crudely frank, quick-witted, generous, ever-thankful for his destiny and a true friend of more name athletes, I expect, than any "layman" that ever lived.

Gene Leone, a mild man briskly efficient, with his location near Madison Square Garden, preceded Shor's as a sports hangout. But Leone's serves only dinner, and after one of those it's not only too late for most sportswriters to do their work, but they're so full they can't get within reaching distance of a typewriter.

Since Damon Runyon's death, the most "Broadway" of the New York sportswriters is Jimmy Cannon of the *Post*. A bachelor, he lives right on Times Square in an Edison Hotel sub-penthouse. While Jimmy composes a heavy run of "think" pieces, frequently indignant and sometimes melancholy, he is the envy of numerous brethren for his talent of producing regular columns of accumulated one-sentence opinions, indictments, preferences, allergies, confessions, drollery and cynical philosophy under the heading, "Nobody Asked Me, But —" or "Do Me A Favor, And —".

Joe Williams, who appears in all Scripps-Howard newspapers, devotes each Monday's space to an unrelated assortment of notes and short items. Joe makes it look easy— but he's a genius at weaving the fragments together smoothly, injecting wise-cracks and barbs.

A famous athlete once expressed an interest in John Lardner's column, and Lardner told him the work was easier than it looked. "Impossible!" was the athlete's comment.

I use miscellaneous brief items the easiest way—just put a few of them together at the bottom of the column almost every day. Whenever possible, I conclude with the nostalgic question: "What ever became of ———?" The blank has been filled with such used-to-be's as watch fobs, umbrella stands, buggy whips, rumble seats, slingshots, gourds, elastic sleeve holders, cherry phosphates, hoboes, shoe buttoners, pen wipers, collapsible tin drinking cups, Wrongway Corrigan and Mysterious Montague. Here's where the mail comes in so helpfully. Readers supply practically all this type of material, and sometimes the mail provides an entire column.

224

What is funny in cold type? Who knows, for sure? All I can go by is what makes me laugh. But there's always the danger that an anecdote new to me is old to the reader.

Sometimes I think newspapers would be smart to shift sportswriters around as the Methodist churches do their preachers. In a new locality before a new congregation, the columnist could re-use some of his old texts. Yet this could be risky, too. The Reverend Harry H. Kruener, Dean of the Chapel at Denison University in Ohio, told me of a dear little old lady waiting for him after church services one Sunday who said: "Dr. Kruener, every sermon you preach is better than the next one."

A columnist can go downhill even faster than a preacher. He doesn't have so far to fall, but every day there's "the next one" to write. Once it's written, though, the man who appreciates his job, and knows he's staying with happiness, feels like saying to his newspaper audience each day: "Welcome. It's so nice of you to come. Here's a draft of something I hope you'll find refreshing."

A Sportswriter's Well-Thumbed Rulebook

RULE 1. Tie goes to the runner. Favor the positive side over the negative.

RULE 2. A man who keeps up with athletes needs to keep in shape. It's amazing how the body responds to a little kindness.

RULE 3. The sportswriter can be on the side of the home team only if he still has an unobscured view of the visiting team's virtues.

RULE 4. Don't call it luck if it was an example of preparation meeting opportunity.

RULE 5. The breaks will be about even in the long run because life is 50-50. Some times things get so bad they can't get any worse, then turn and get better. Then they get so good they can't get any better, so they turn for worse.

RULE 6. It is better to travel hopefully than to arrive. The start of every game is exciting. The finish of few are.

RULE 7. Anybody can see trouble ahead if he looks down the road far enough. Play today's game today.

RULE 8. Try to function in disaster. Try to finish in style.

RULE 9. If Rules 1 through 8 do not cover the situation, quote Bill Corum's opinion: "Since none of us goes by the reviewing stand save once, it might be that the way to pass the judges is laughing."

RULE 10. Don't ever call the game on account of darkness. Instead, brighten your outlook by remembering Grantland Rice's poem about sportswriters:

If somebody whispered to me—"You can have your pick,"
If kind fortune came to woo me, where the gold was thick,
I would still, by hill and hollow, round the world away,
Stirring deeds of contest follow, till I'm bent and gray.

Sport is youth—and youth's eternal, where the flame is bright;
And our hearts will still be vernal when our hair is white.
And though wealth may never love us, say that we have seen
That the sky is blue above us, and the turf is green.

Index

229

230

235